VOLUME 14

EZEKIEL and DANIEL

Linda B. Hinton

ABINGDON PRESS
Nashville

D1157397

EZEKIEL AND DANIEL

Copyright © 1988 by Graded Press

This book is printed on recycled, acid-free paper.

Library of Congress Cataloging-in-Publication Data

Cokesbury basic Bible commentary.
    Basic Bible commentary / by Linda B. Hinton . . . [et al.].
        p. cm.
    Originally published: Cokesbury basic Bible commentary. Nashville: Graded Press, © 1988.
    ISBN 0-687-02620-2 (pbk. : v. 1: alk. paper)
    1. Bible—Commentaries. I. Hinton, Linda B. II. Title.
[BS491.2.C65   1994]
220.7—dc20   94-10965
                                                                                        CIP

ISBN 0-687-02633-4 (v. 14, Ezekiel–Daniel)
ISBN 0-687-02620-2 (v. 1, Genesis)
ISBN 0-687-02621-0 (v. 2, Exodus–Leviticus)
ISBN 0-687-02622-9 (v. 3, Numbers–Deuteronomy)
ISBN 0-687-02623-7 (v. 4, Joshua–Ruth)
ISBN 0-687-02624-5 (v. 5, 1–2 Samuel)
ISBN 0-687-02625-3 (v. 6, 1–2 Kings)
ISBN 0-687-02626-1 (v. 7, 1–2 Chronicles)
ISBN 0-687-02627-X (v. 8, Ezra–Esther)
ISBN 0-687-02628-8 (v. 9, Job)
ISBN 0-687-02629-6 (v. 10, Psalms)
ISBN 0-687-02630-X (v. 11, Proverbs–Song of Solomon)
ISBN 0-687-02631-8 (v. 12, Isaiah)
ISBN 0-687-02632-6 (v. 13, Jeremiah–Lamentations)
ISBN 0-687-02634-2 (v. 15, Hosea–Jonah)
ISBN 0-687-02635-0 (v. 16, Micah–Malachi)
ISBN 0-687-02636-9 (v. 17, Matthew)
ISBN 0-687-02637-7 (v. 18, Mark)
ISBN 0-687-02638-5 (v. 19, Luke)
ISBN 0-687-02639-3 (v. 20, John)
ISBN 0-687-02640-7 (v. 21, Acts)
ISBN 0-687-02642-3 (v. 22, Romans)
ISBN 0-687-02643-1 (v. 23, 1–2 Corinthians)
ISBN 0-687-02644-X (v. 24, Galatians–Ephesians)
ISBN 0-687-02645-8 (v. 25, Philippians–2 Thessalonians)
ISBN 0-687-02646-6 (v. 26, 1 Timothy–Philemon)
ISBN 0-687-02647-4 (v. 27, Hebrews)
ISBN 0-687-02648-2 (v. 28, James–Jude)
ISBN 0-687-02649-0 (v. 29, Revelation)
ISBN 0-687-02650-4 (complete set of 29 vols.)

94 95 96 97 98 99 00 01 02 03 — 10 9 8 7 6 5 4 3 2 1

MANUFACTURED IN THE UNITED STATES OF AMERICA

Contents

Outline of Ezekiel and Daniel

The Book of Ezekiel

I. Introduction and Ezekiel's Call to Prophesy (1:1–3:21)
  A. Introduction (1:1-3)
  B. Vision of the glory of God (1:4–3:15)
  C. Commission as watchman (3:16-21)
II. Judgment Against Judah and Jerusalem (3:22–24:27)
  A. The siege of Jerusalem (3:22–5:17)
  B. Announcements of judgment (6:1–7:27)
  C. The Temple vision (8:1–11:25)
  D. Symbolic acts: the Exile and judgment (12:1–14:23)
  E. Concerning unfaithfulness and sin (15:1–20:49)
  F. Prophecies of punishment (21:1–23:49)
  G. Oracles concerning the siege of Jerusalem (24:1-27)
III. Judgment Against Foreign Nations (25:1–32:32)
  A. Ammon, Moab, Edom, and the Philistines (25:1-17)
  B. Tyre (26:1–28:26)
  C. Egypt (29:1–32:32)
IV. Oracles of Responsibility and Justice (33:1-33)
V. Restoration and Salvation (34:1–39:29)
VI. Vision of the Restored Land and Temple (40:1–48:35)
  A. The new Temple (40:1–46:24)
  B. The life-giving river (47:1-12)
  C. Division of the land of Israel (47:13–48:35)

The Book of Daniel

I. Daniel and His Friends in Babylon (1:1–6:28)
   A. Daniel, Shadrach, Meshach, and Abednego (1:1-21)
   B. Nebuchadnezzar's dream of a great image (2:1-49)
   C. The fiery furnace (3:1-30)
   D. Story of Nebuchadnezzar's madness (4:1-37)
   E. Story of the handwriting on the wall (5:1-31)
   F. Daniel in the lions' den (6:1-28)
II. Daniel's Visions (7:1–12:13)
   A. Vision of the four beasts (7:1-28)
   B. Vision of the ram and the he-goat (8:1-27)
   C. Daniel's prayer (9:1-27)
   D. Vision by the great river (10:1–11:1)
   E. Revelation of the future (11:2-45)
   F. The time of the end (12:1-13)

Historical Background

After the death of King Solomon, the kingdom of Israel was divided into Israel in the North and Judah in the South. (*Israel* sometimes means specifically the Northern Kingdom. Israel can also mean the people of Israel, which includes both the northern and the southern kingdoms.) The Northern Kingdom was conquered by Assyria in 722 B.C.

When Assyria's power declined, King Josiah of Judah (640–609 B.C.) extended his power into parts of the Northern Kingdom. Josiah's reign ended when he was killed in a battle with the Egyptians at Megiddo in 609 B.C. His son, Jehoahaz, took his place as king, but the Egyptians took him to Egypt and put his brother, Jehoiakim, on the throne in Judah.

During this time, Egypt and Babylonia were fighting over what was left of the Assyrian Empire. In 605 B.C. the Babylonians defeated the Egyptians in a key battle at Carchemish, and Judah then came under Babylonian influence. Daniel and his friends are said to have been taken into exile in Babylonia at this time (see Daniel 1).

King Jehoiakim tried to break away from Babylonian control in 601 B.C. to establish Judah as an independent state once again. In December, 598 B.C., the Babylonian army besieged Jerusalem. Jehoiakim was killed and his son, Jehoiachin, soon surrendered the city. Hundreds of Israelites were taken as prisoners to Babylon, including the king, his court, priests, artisans, and other leading citizens. Ezekiel was in this group of exiles. Zedekiah,

Jehoiachin's uncle, was made king under Babylonian control. Judah rebelled in 588 B.C., and, once again, Babylonian forces attacked Jerusalem. The city fell in 587 B.C. after an eighteen-month siege. More Israelites were taken to Babylon and Jerusalem was destroyed. King Nebuchadnezzar of Babylon appointed Gedaliah, a member of a prominent Judean family, as governor of Judah. Gedaliah was killed in 582 B.C. by a zealous member of the Judean royal family. More captives were taken from Judah to Babylon, and the hardships of those left in Judah increased.

In 539 B.C. Persia defeated Babylonia. Cyrus, the Persian king, gave the exiled Israelites permission to return to Judah. The Israelites continued to live under Persian rule until Persia was defeated by the Greeks under Alexander the Great in 334 B.C.

Judah rebelled against Greek rule in 165 B.C. and was an independent nation until Roman legions captured Jerusalem in 63 B.C.

Important Dates for Ezekiel and Daniel

609–598 B.C.—Jehoiakim king of Judah

605 B.C.—Babylonians defeat Egyptians and Assyrians at Carchemish, extend influence over Judah; Daniel in Babylon

605–562 B.C.—Nebuchadnezzar king of Babylon

597 B.C.—Babylonians capture Jerusalem; many Israelites taken to Babylon, including Ezekiel

597–587 B.C.—Zedekiah king of Judah

587 B.C.—Jerusalem destroyed by Babylonians; more Israelites taken into exile

556–539 B.C.—Nabonidus king of Babylon, Belshazzar acts as king for ten years in his absence

550/549–539 B.C. (approximately)—Belshazzar rules for Nabonidus in Babylon; setting for Daniel 7 and 8

539 B.C.—Babylonia defeated by the Persians

550–529 B.C.—Cyrus king of Persia

334–331 B.C.—Conquests of Alexander the Great of Greece; Persia defeated

323 B.C.—Death of Alexander; Greek empire divided

323–164 B.C.—Judah under Greek rule

170 B.C. (approximately)—Rome the rising world power

165/164 B.C.—Jewish rebels take control of Judah from Greeks

Introduction to Ezekiel

Ezekiel was a prophet of Israel whose ministry and words are recorded in the book which bears his name. His call to prophesy came in 593 B.C. when he was living in exile in Babylonia. He fulfilled his prophetic duties in exile and probably never returned to his homeland.

The events of 597 B.C. had thrown Israel into a crisis that was both political and spiritual. With their humiliation and defeat at the hands of the Babylonians the people of Israel began to question God's power to control events in history. They also questioned God's faithfulness to the promises made to Israel in the past.

Ezekiel dealt with these disturbing questions. His prophecies answered these questions according to God's power, justice, and mercy. Ezekiel's prophecy showed the people of Israel how to understand what had happened to them and how to find their way into the future as God's chosen people.

Ezekiel the Book

The book of Ezekiel is a collection of prophetic speeches and vision reports. Ezekiel's speeches (also called oracles) are announcements (through the prophet) of God's word for Israel. Ezekiel announces judgment and punishment for Israel's sins. He also announces God's promises of restoration and salvation for the people.

The collection of Ezekiel's prophecies may be divided into three major sections. Chapters 1–24 are mainly announcements of judgment against Jerusalem from 593 B.C. (the time of Ezekiel's call to prophecy) to 587 B.C. (the destruction of Jerusalem). Chapters 25–32 are announcements of judgment against foreign nations from approximately 587–585 B.C. (except 29:17-21, from 571 B.C.). Chapters 33–48 are prophecies about the future restoration of Israel, which come after 587 B.C.

Ezekiel's prophecies were collected and preserved, either orally or in writing. This was probably first done by Ezekiel himself and a group of his followers. This collection was eventually organized and edited into the form we know today.

Ezekiel the Man

Ezekiel was born into a priestly family and may have been trained for the priesthood. He was probably taken from Jerusalem to Babylon in 597 B.C. along with other Temple priests. We do not know how old he was at the time, but he may have been a young adult. As far as we know he spent the rest of his life in Babylonia.

Once in Babylon, Ezekiel settled with other exiles in a village away from the capital and lived in humble circumstances. His wife went with him into exile. She died in Babylonia, leaving Ezekiel numb and speechless with grief.

The spectacular vision in which Ezekiel was called to prophesy (see Ezekiel 1:1–3:15) reflects the strength and turbulance of his prophetic ministry. The power and thunder of God's might echo in Ezekiel's life and words. Ezekiel showed self-discipline and strong emotion as he fulfilled the duties God set before him. He was both stern and passionate in his commitment to proclaim and to act out God's word for Israel.

Ezekiel's ministry did not come without a personal cost to the prophet. He suffered misunderstanding and sometimes outright hostility for the message he brought. His actions at times may have seemed bizarre to his fellow exiles. Even his wife's death and the great loss he felt were used by God as part of his message. He shared physically and emotionally in the despair and hardship of exiled Israelites.

Ezekiel was more than just a "fellow sufferer," however. His message about Israel's sin and its consequences helped the people of Israel make sense out of what had happened to them. Ezekiel provided answers to the inevitable questions of "Why?" and "Where do we go from here?"

Ezekiel 1–3

Introduction to These Chapters

Ezekiel 1-3 introduces the book and establishes Ezekiel's authority as a prophet. These chapters describe the visions in which God calls Ezekiel to prophesy and commissions Ezekiel as a watchman for Israel.

Here is an outline of these chapters.

I. Vision of the Glory of the Lord (1:1-28)
   A. Introduction (1:1-3)
   B. Signs of God's presence (1:4)
   C. The living creatures (1:5-14)
   D. The wheel within a wheel (1:15-25)
   E. The glory of the Lord (1:26-28)
II. God Commissions Ezekiel as a Messenger (2:1–3:27)
   A. Ezekiel's task (2:1-7)
   B. Ezekiel accepts his task (2:8–3:3)
   C. Ezekiel is fortified (3:4-11)
   D. The effects of the vision (3:12-15)
   E. Ezekiel's commission as a watchman (3:16-21)
   F. Ezekiel is bound by God's word (3:22-27)

Introduction (1:1-3)

In the thirtieth year may refer to Ezekiel's age when he was called to be a prophet. Or it may refer to the thirtieth year after Ezekiel's call when his prophecies may have been collected in writing for the first time.

The date given in verse 1 is explained more fully by the editor in verse 2. The fifth year of the exile of King

Jehoiachin is the year 593 B.C. These dates are based on a lunar calendar with the beginning of the year in the spring. Thus Ezekiel's vision came on or about July 31, 593 B.C.

Through the power of God Ezekiel sees a vision. He is shown a dimension of reality that human beings normally do not see or hear.

In verse 3 the editor establishes Ezekiel's lineage and tells where he lives. The editor also testifies to the authority of Ezekiel's prophecy by telling us that *the hand of the LORD was on him there.*

Signs of God's Presence (1:4)

Wind, cloud, and fire come with the appearance of God on earth (see also 1 Kings 19:11-12; Exodus 19:16). *Out of the north* may reflect the view that God's dwelling is in the north (see Psalm 48:2).

The Living Creatures (1:5-14)

The creatures are probably cherubim, who are heavenly beings associated with God's presence and with sacred areas (see also Genesis 3:24; Exodus 25:18-20; Revelation 4:6-7). They are mentioned throughout Scripture and take many different forms.

The Wheel Within a Wheel (1:15-25)

The *wheel within* (NRSV) or *wheel intersecting a wheel* (NIV) may have been two wheels set at right angles to each other.

Chrysolite (NIV) or *beryl* (NRSV) is a gemstone which is usually olive-green in color.

The four creatures and the four wheels work together. They may move in any direction, even to the four corners of the earth, wherever the spirit leads them.

The eyes in the wheels suggest God's ability to see and know all that happens.

In Hebrew thought, the firmament is the division

which forms the sky between the upper waters and the waters of the earth (see Genesis 1:6-8). The living creatures move under the radiant likeness of such a firmament. This firmament in turn supports God's throne in the vision.

The Glory of the Lord 1:26-28

Ezekiel sees forms which are like, or similar to, God and God's throne. The radiance of these forms is like that of gems, metal, fire, and rainbows.

Ezekiel sees the likeness of God's glory. The Hebrew word for glory is *kabod*. *Kabod* means weight or importance, and this word is often used in the Old Testament to describe the form of God's presence (see also Psalm 19:1; Isaiah 66:18). Used in this context, the appearance of God's glory expresses God's complete power and holiness.

Ezekiel's Task (2:1-7)

Son of man (NIV) or *mortal* (NRSV), or *Ben-adam* in Hebrew, means human being. Though he is only a lowly mortal, Ezekiel is called to serve and be in relationship with the Lord of all creation.

God tells Ezekiel that he is to speak God's word to the people of Israel: *say to them, "Thus says the Lord GOD"* (NRSV) or *"This is what the Sovereign LORD says"* (NIV). God is sending Ezekiel to speak because the people of Israel . . . have *"rebelled against me."*

Ezekiel Accepts His Task (2:8–3:3)

God warns Ezekiel that a prophet must be obedient to God's call. The words of lamentation and mourning on the scroll offered to Ezekiel are symbolic of the words he must speak to Israel.

By eating the scroll, Ezekiel accepts God's commissioning of him as a prophet, and he surrenders himself to God's will. The creative power of God's word is thus transferred to the prophet. This action also suggests that God's word is as necessary as food for the survival of God's people.

Ezekiel Is Fortified (3:4-11)

God tells Ezekiel that even foreigners would be more receptive to God's word than the people of Israel. Nevertheless, Ezekiel is to be more stubborn in his prophecy than the people are in their resistance to it. The face is the part of the body through which a person's attitudes and character are most often expressed. Ezekiel's hard face expresses his determination and lack of fear in the face of Israel's rebelliousness.

Ezekiel is to receive God's words into his ears and his heart. In the Old Testament, a person's heart is seen as the source of energy and of the thoughts, attitudes, hopes, fears, and desires which make up a person's character. Thus Ezekiel is to take God's word into the very core of his being.

The Effects of the Vision (3:12-15)

Acceptance of a call to prophesy is not to be taken lightly. As other prophets before him (see for example, Jeremiah 1:5-8; 15:10-12), Ezekiel feels the burden of his call. The Hebrew word that is translated *overwhelmed* (NIV) or *stunned* (NRSV) comes from a root word which means to devastate, to stun, or to amaze. Ezekiel may have been speechless and motionless for seven days after his vision.

Ezekiel's Commission as a Watchman (3:16-21)

God appoints Ezekiel as a watchman for the people of Israel. He must warn them about their wickedness just as the watchman of a city must raise an alarm should an enemy approach. Failure to raise an alarm could cost innocent lives. Thus Ezekiel is liable for any innocent blood lost in sin should he fail to deliver his message of warning.

A *stumbling block* is an obstacle that causes someone's downfall. Elsewhere in Ezekiel, idols are such an obstacle to Israel (see Ezekiel 7:19; 14:3). God may place such an obstacle in someone's path (perhaps as a test) or God may be the obstacle for the disobedient (see Isaiah 8:14).

Ezekiel Is Bound by God's Word (3:22-27)

Ezekiel again sees the overwhelming glory of God. The *plain* (NIV) or *valley* (NRSV) is the southern Tigris-Euphrates valley. God will control the timing as well as the content of Ezekiel's message. Ezekiel will stay in his home and be silent (though perhaps not tied with literal cords) until God opens his mouth. When Ezekiel does deliver his prophecies to the people, each person will be responsible for receiving or rejecting his message.

§ § § § § § §

The Message of Ezekiel 1–3

The vision reports of Ezekiel 1–3 establish the perspective that Ezekiel's message comes from God. What do these visions tell us about God's word and its relationship to God's people?

§ Genesis 1 tells us that God's word has creative power. According to Old Testament tradition, this creative power extends to God's word spoken by the prophet. The prophetic word about the future is not spoken to speculate about or to predict the future but to make known God's word for the future. The prophetic word acts to make things happen.

§ The Israelites believed that oracles and demonstrations of God's words possessed a power that set in motion the accomplishment of God's word. Language was seen as a dynamic force that could affect the physical world. Thus, the prophetic future began with the spoken word or symbolic action of the prophet on God's behalf.

§ In the past, the people of Israel knew their homeland as God's land. They knew God's special presence in Jerusalem and in the holy of holies in the Temple. Yet, God meets Ezekiel in an unclean, foreign land. This shows God's willingness and power to meet the people wherever they are. God shows Ezekiel and, through Ezekiel, shows Israel that God is free to act and to be in relationship with Israel anywhere.

§ Each individual is responsible for recognizing God's truth as it comes through the prophet. Individual salvation as well as the salvation of Israel as a whole is at stake in Ezekiel's message.

§ § § § § § §

Ezekiel 4–7

Introduction to These Chapters

Ezekiel 4–7 contains reports of symbolic actions and announcements of judgment. Ezekiel acts out the coming siege of Jerusalem and tells the people the cost of their sin.

Here is an outline of these chapters.

Hardships of the Siege (4:1-17)

Ezekiel's actions are symbolic of the fate of the people of Jerusalem and of the city. The interpretation of these actions serves as a sign or message to the exiles and to the people still in Jerusalem.

Verses 1-3: Ezekiel uses a sun-dried brick with a drawing of Jerusalem on it to act out what will happen when the Babylonians lay siege to Jerusalem again. The Babylonians had besieged Jerusalem in 597 B.C. and would do so again in 587 B.C. because of Judah's rebellion. The people refused to accept their punishment by God through Babylon and continued in their sin. The iron plate is a symbol of God's steadfast will to punish the sinful people of Jerusalem.

Verses 4-8: Ezekiel symbolically bears the guilt and punishment of Israel and of Judah. The total of 430 days corresponds to the 430 years Israel spent in slavery in Egypt (see Exodus 12:40).

Verses 9-17: Mixing of different kinds of food and rationing food and water symbolize the hardships of the coming siege. Some people in Jerusalem eventually resorted to cannibalism and many starved to death (see Jeremiah 19:9; Lamentations 2:19-20).

God allows Ezekiel about one-half pound of bread per day, to be cooked either on a hot stone or directly in hot ashes. He is allowed about one and three-fourths pints of water per day.

Baking food on human dung represents the unclean food which the people will have to eat. Ezekiel protests this instruction because he wants to keep the rules of cleanliness he learned as part of his priestly duties (see Deuteronomy 23:12-14; Leviticus 11:39; Exodus 22:30-31).

The Sword of the Lord (5:1-17)

Ezekiel acts out the fate of those still in Jerusalem and then gives the reasons for this punishment.

Verses 1-4: The sword used as a razor represents military defeat for Jerusalem. Being shaved symbolizes defeat and loss of dignity (see Isaiah 7:20; 2 Samuel 10:4-5). The symbolism of verses 2-4 is explained in verse 12.

The hair which is bound in Ezekiel's shirts is the exiles, those whom God will *scatter* to the wind. Even they, however, will not all be safe from the sword and the fire which are God's judgment.

The Hebrew word for center is *navel.* Jerusalem was a holy city, believed to be the geographical and spiritual center of the world. The city will be destroyed, however, because of the people's sin. They have rebelled against obeying God's law (*ordinances* [NRSV] or *laws* [NIV] and *statutes* [NRSV] or *decrees* [NIV]) which is part of the covenant relationship (see Deuteronomy 5:1-21).

Israel has broken her sacred law and covenant oath; therefore God will punish her. *Abominations* (NRSV) or *detestable idols* (NIV) are anything associated with idolatry. *Detestable things* (NRSV) or *practices* (NIV) are objects used in the worship of idols.

Verses 13-17: Israel was to have been a source of blessing to the nations (see Genesis 12:1-3). Now the nations will look on in horror at what has happened to God's chosen people. Israel will face the sword, famine, wild beasts, and disease (in Jerusalem, Jeremiah was saying the same thing, see Jeremiah 24:9-10).

They shall know that I, the LORD, have spoken (verse 13) explains a purpose behind Israel's punishment beyond the execution of divine justice. This purpose is that the people of Israel will come to know God. Such knowledge is an important part of Ezekiel's message. Through a new knowledge of God will come new obedience and new life.

Judgment on Idolatry (6:1-14)

Verses 1-10: These verses are an oracle, or message, of judgment against the mountains of Israel. The mountains were often sites of the *high places* of pagan worship. These were open-air sanctuaries with incense altars, statues, trees, or other objects sacred to such idol worship.

To set one's face is an expression of hostility. God's hostile face acts on the mountains through Ezekiel's actions and words.

Idol worship is a sign of the people's alienation from God, and the mountains hold the symbols of this alienation. In Hebrew, the word which Ezekiel uses for idols is a pun on the word for dung.

Verses 8-10: There is hope of escape for some Israelites so that they may remember and know God. To remember is to be open to and seek after God. To know God is not just mental but also involves the heart, which is the inner being.

Verses 11-14: Ezekiel proclaims that not only the people will suffer for their sins but the land itself will also be wasted. The consequences of sin are far-reaching.

From the wilderness to Riblah (NRSV) or *desert to Diblah* (NIV) means from the southern to the northern borders of greater Israel.

The Coming Judgment (7:1-9)

Chapter 7 contains announcements of judgment concerning the day of the Lord in which the land of Israel will come to an end.

Verses 1-4, 5-9: The end is a catastrophe for Israel (see also Amos 8:2). Because of sin, God's wrath brings death, dishonor, and desolation to the people and the land.

At one time the day of the Lord was believed to be a day when God would act against Israel's enemies. The prophet Amos warned the Israelites, however, that they could become God's enemies because of their sin. The day of the Lord would, thus, be one of darkness and defeat for them as well. Ezekiel also sees this day as an end for Israel, not a day of salvation. This end is a specific historical event which is foreseen, in this case, in the destruction of Jerusalem by the Babylonians in 587 B.C.

In the events of this awful day, God will be revealed to the people of Israel.

What Will Happen in Jerusalem (7:10-23)

Verses 10-13: Just as the day will not be as people expect it to be, so also will normal human relationships be upset. The fruit of their sin is injustice, pride, and violence. Now they will reap the harvest of God's righteous anger.

Verses 14-23: God's wrath (righteous anger) upsets their plans for battle. The trumpet calls the soldiers to defend their city, but it will do no good. They mourn their dead and are disgraced (verse 18).

The people had made their gold and silver into idols which are *the stumbling block of their iniquity* (NRSV) or which *made them stumble into sin* (NIV) . . . *their abominable images* (NRSV) or *detestable idols* (NIV), *their detestable things* (NRSV) or *vile images* (NIV) (verses 19-20). These idols will not save them from hunger or from the enemy. The *wicked of the earth* (verse 21) and the *worst* (NRSV) or *wicked* (NIV) *of the nations* (verse 24) are the Babylonians.

The *treasured* or secret place is the Temple or the holy of holies in the Temple.

The People Are Judged (7:23-27)

The normal channels of wisdom and guidance will be closed to the people. Even their leaders will be paralyzed with fear. Too late will they seek peace. Peace is not just an absence of conflict but is a state of wholeness. Peace means physical and mental well-being, prosperity, right relationships among people, and right relationships between the people and God.

As the people of Israel have lived, so shall they be judged.

§ § § § § § §

The Message of Ezekiel 4–7

God is the judge in the court in which Israel is tried, and Ezekiel's announcements of judgment to Israel reflect Israel's legal heritage. A case is made against Israel and the resulting judgment is announced. Prophetic announcements of judgment typically have three parts (see, for example, Ezekiel 5:5-8):

- call to attention (verse 5)
- description of sins (verses 6-7)
- announcement of punishment (verse 8)

Sometimes these parts are in a different order or are mixed (see for example, Ezekiel 6:1-4).

The phrase *Thus says the LORD* (NRSV) or *This is what the Sovereign LORD says* (NIV) or the word *Behold* often begins Ezekiel's announcements of judgment. The word *Therefore* often begins the part of the speech in which punishment is announced. The phrase they shall *know that I am the LORD* ends many of Ezekiel's messages.

Thus within each oracle a case is made against Israel. The basis of Israelite law is the Law (Torah) which is the supreme revelation of God's will. This Law is the foundation on which the covenant community is built. Therefore, the Law is vital to Israel's survival as a people.

Ezekiel's announcements of judgment make a connection between the Law and what has happened to Israel.

§ The Israelites' subjugation to the Babylonians, their exile, and the coming destruction of Jerusalem are not random acts of fate. These tragedies are logical and faithful extensions of their failure to live under the Law.

§ The Law is at work, and, therefore, God is at work in their lives.

§ God is revealed to Israel even in judgment.

§ § § § § § §

Ezekiel 8–11

Introduction to These Chapters

On approximately September 17, 592 B.C., Ezekiel is
transported from Babylon to Jerusalem in a vision.
Chapters 8–11 tell of this vision.
Here is an outline of these chapters.
  I. Abominations in the Temple (8:1-18)
     A. From Tel-Abib to the Temple (8:1-4)
     B. The image of jealousy (8:5-6)
     C. Elders caught in idol worship (8:7-13)
     D. More abominations (8:14-18)
 II. The Guilty Are Killed (9:1-11)
III. God Leaves the Temple (10:1-22)
 IV. Prophecies of Judgment and Promise (11:1-25)
     A. Prophecy against wicked counselors (11:1-12)
     B. A word of hope (11:13-21)
     C. God's glory leaves Jerusalem (11:22-25)

From Tel-Abib to the Temple (8:1-4)

Elders among the exiles had perhaps come to Ezekiel
for guidance (see also Ezekiel 20:1). This vision, which
Ezekiel later tells them about (see 11:25), may have come
to Ezekiel in response to their questions. The spirit of
God falls upon the prophet and he sees the form of God's
glory.

Ezekiel travels with God to Jerusalem and finds
himself at the third gate which leads from the king's
palace into the Temple area.

The *seat* (NRSV: which is only implied in the NIV) is a

hollow area in the wall of the gateway where statues or other religious figures are placed. The *image of jealousy* (NRSV) is an idol which provokes God's jealousy (see Exodus 20:5).

The Image of Jealousy (8:5-6)

This image may have been a statue of Tammuz (see verse 14) which had been moved to the altar gate. Tammuz is the Mesopotamian god of vegetation.

Some Israelites have brought the worship of foreign gods into the Temple, perhaps combining this idolatry with worship of God (see also Jeremiah 11:13). Their idolatry will cause God to abandon the Temple.

Elders Caught in Idol Worship (8:7-13)

Ezekiel sees seventy elders, the traditional representatives of the people of Israel, worshiping idols. The images on the walls are of creatures which Israel is forbidden to eat (see Leviticus 11), much less to worship. This worship service may have been similar to those held for the Egyptian sun god, Osiris.

The elders commit these abominations because they no longer believe that God is present in Israel. They fail to see God's hand in what has happened to them, so they fall further into sin.

More Abominations (8:14-18)

The women mourn for Tammuz, who dies during the dry months (approximately mid-June to mid-September) and who comes back to life bringing fruitfulness to the earth during the wet months (approximately mid-October to mid-April).

The men (verse 16) have literally and figuratively turned their backs on God as they worship the sun. As if their idolatry isn't enough to alienate them from God, they are also guilty of injustice and violence to one another (see also 7:23).

The *branch* may refer to a kind of vine-sprout that is used in some pagan rites. *Putting the branch to their nose* may be a saying which means to insult or "turn one's nose up" at God.

The Guilty Are Killed (9:1-11)

Six divine executioners are called to carry out Jerusalem's punishment.

The man clothed in linen is also a heavenly figure. He is God's scribe who marks those people who grieve for the sins of their brothers and sisters. Linen is a ritually clean fabric (as opposed to wool which comes from an animal). Linen is worn by priests and angels.

The bronze altar may be one which was put in the Temple by King Solomon.

The sun-worshiping elders are the first to be slain. Their dead bodies are unclean and make the Temple unclean (see Numbers 19:11-16).

Ezekiel cries out on behalf of the people of Israel. God responds by again telling of Israel's crimes. Their social and religious sins are part of the same problem: They no longer have a right relationship with God.

The scribe's report in verse 11 implies that those with the mark have been spared.

God Leaves the Temple (10:1-22)

Chapter 10 adds details to the basic vision report which continues in 10:2, 4, 7, 18, 19.

The man in linen is instructed to take coals from between the cherubim which support God's throne and scatter the coals over the city of Jerusalem. Thus will Jerusalem be consumed in the holy fire of God's judgment.

The *glory of the* LORD shows God's overwhelming majesty and God's presence with the people. God's glory moves to the east gate of the Temple before leaving the city (11:23).

Prophecy Against Wicked Counselors (11:1-12)

Verses 1-3: The leaders are telling people not to build houses, perhaps in areas outside Jerusalem's walls. They may do this in hopes of later having the land for themselves (see verse 15).

Iniquity (NRSV) or *evil* (NIV) and *wicked counsel* (NRSV) or *wicked advice* (NIV) may also refer to plots among King Zedekiah's advisers to rebel against Babylon.

The men at the gate speak of Jerusalem as a cauldron, that is, as protection for the people within the walls. They are the *meat,* a valuable commodity in these hard times.

Verses 4-12: Ezekiel prophesies that the only protected flesh in Jerusalem will be those who have already been killed.

The rebellious Israelites will be taken out of Jerusalem by the Babylonians who will execute God's judgment on Israel. The border(s) may refer to Riblah, a town on the old northern border of Israel (see Jeremiah 52:24-27).

Because Israel rejected God's law to follow the gods of other nations, Israel will be destroyed by another nation.

A Word of Hope (11:13-21)

One of the wicked counselors dies during Ezekiel's prophecy (see also 1 Kings 13:20-24), perhaps as a sign that the coming punishment is sure. This causes Ezekiel to again plead with God on Israel's behalf.

Verses 14-21: God assures Ezekiel that there is hope for the Israelites in exile. Some people in Jerusalem believe that the exiles have gone far away from the Lord because they have left Judah and the Temple where God's presence has been in the past. Those left in Jerusalem believe the exiles have given up any connection with the land and with God.

Ezekiel proclaims, however, that God is a *sanctuary* for a while to the exiles. Even in exile the people may worship and seek God.

When the exiles are returned to Israel they (and those in Jerusalem who were marked and spared) will cleanse the land and the Temple. God will then cleanse them and renew the covenant with them (verses 19-20; see also Leviticus 26:12; Jeremiah 32:38).

The *heart* symbolizes the will (voluntary) and the *spirit* symbolizes emotion or temperament (involuntary). These basic aspects of human nature will be brought under God's direction. Their hard hearts which rebelled against God (see 3:7) will be replaced by a truly human heart of flesh, as they were created to have.

God's Glory Leaves Jerusalem (11:22-25)

God's glory leaves the Temple and the city to stand upon the Mount of Olives. The judgment of Jerusalem is now complete.

Ezekiel is taken in the vision back to his home. Once the vision leaves him he is able to tell the exiles the word which he has seen and heard.

§ § § § § § §

The Message of Ezekiel 8–11

With this vision Ezekiel and the exiles are allowed to see the consequences of sin within their beloved Temple and home city. Jerusalem and the Temple are the centers of their spiritual and physical yearnings for home. Yet, God shows them that they may not count on even this sacred ground from now on. Above all, the prophet and people are shown God's freedom to act according to the divine will. What does this vision tell us about the freedom of God?

§ God's presence in the Temple is not guaranteed. God will leave the Temple and the city because of human sin.

§ God will meet the exiles in a land far from their traditional place of worship. God is now the sanctuary for their prayers and obedience.

§ Israel must endure disaster as the consequence of sin but will not be completely rejected. God is free both to judge and to redeem. Therefore, the people of Israel will be recreated with new hearts and spirits.

§ § § § § § §

Ezekiel 12–15

Introduction to These Chapters

Chapters 12–15 contain reports of symbolic actions and oracles addressed to the exiles and to those still in Jerusalem.

Here is an outline of these chapters.

I. Israel Is a Rebellious House (12:1-28)
  A. They shall go into exile (12:1-16)
  B. The fearfulness of the siege (12:17-20)
  C. False sayings (12:21-28)
II. Condemnation of False Prophets (13:1-23)
  A. Foxes among the ruins (13:1-9)
  B. A whitewashed wall (13:10-16)
  C. False prophecy and magic (13:17-23)
III. Idolatry and Individual Responsibility (14:1-23)
  A. Idols lead to alienation (14:1-11)
  B. Individual responsibility (14:12-23)
IV. Parable of the Vine (15:1-8)

They Shall Go into Exile (12:1-16)

Ezekiel acts out an exile's journey in front of his fellow exiles, and then explains to them what his actions mean.

Verses 1-7: The exiles, as well as those still in Jerusalem, rebel against God. They must be made to understand the truth of what is happening to them. These verses relate directly to the political and religious situation in Jerusalem and among the exiles at this time.

This symbolic action by Ezekiel and its interpretation may have come in 592 or 591 B.C. In Judah, King Zedekiah and his advisers plotted with Egypt and other neighboring countries to rebel against Babylon. Zedekiah's visit to Babylon in 593 B.C. may have been required by Nebuchadnezzar for Zedekiah to reaffirm his loyalty to the Babylonian king.

Zedekiah also sent envoys to Nebuchadnezzar to assure the king of his loyalty. One of these messengers took a letter from the prophet Jeremiah in Jerusalem to the exile community in Babylon (see Jeremiah 29:1-23). In this letter Jeremiah urged the exiles to make a home for themselves in Babylonia and to seek their welfare in Babylon's welfare because it was God's will for them to be there. He warned them against false prophets among their own people who would deceive them (see Jeremiah 29:7-9, 21-23).

Some false prophets among the exiles may have been executed by Nebuchadnezzar because of their plots for rebellion. King Jehoiachin, also an exile, was eventually imprisoned by Nebuchadnezzar, perhaps because of revolutionary activity among the exiles which centered on him.

Though Jeremiah told the people of Israel that Babylon was God's instrument of punishment, he also said that Babylon itself would face God's judgment. In about 594–593 B.C. a collection of his oracles against Babylon was made and was sent to Babylon (see Jeremiah 51:59-64). From these prophecies the exiles may have decided that Babylon's defeat was coming soon.

Both Jeremiah and Ezekiel, however, told the people of Israel that they must first submit to their punishment from God. They must accept their control by the Babylonians and seek a renewed relationship with God. Instead, leaders among the exiles and in Jerusalem continued to plan a military rebellion against Babylon.

Ezekiel's *baggage* (NRSV) or *belongings* (NIV) (verse 4) may contain some food and water, cooking utensils, bedding, and perhaps an extra cloak. Long journeys would begin after the heat of the day had passed so Ezekiel is to go out in the evening.

EZEKIEL AND DANIEL

His breaking through the wall of his house could symbolize a secret escape through a city wall during a siege, or it could symbolize the destruction during a siege. Ezekiel covers his head in shame and suffering at the loss of his homeland.

A *sign* is an act or event that shows God's presence or intentions.

Verses 8-16: The *prince* is a leader, probably King Zedekiah. During the siege of Jerusalem in the summer of 587 B.C. Zedekiah fled the city but was captured by the Babylonians (see also Jeremiah 52:7-10).

More Israelites will be taken into exile. There they will confess their sins and know that God has punished them.

The Fearfulness of the Siege (12:17-20)

Ezekiel takes on the fear and trembling of the people in Jerusalem who will endure the coming siege by the Babylonians (January 588–August 587 B.C.). Because of their violence (see Ezekiel 7:10-12; 9:9-10) they, their city, and their land will be subject to devastating violence.

False Sayings (12:21-28)

In these two oracles (verses 21-25, 26-28) Ezekiel addresses some of the false beliefs held by the people of Israel.

A *proverb* is generally a short saying of popular wisdom.

The people ignore prophetic visions as the years of their captivity wear on. They perhaps feel caught between the prophecies of Ezekiel and Jeremiah and those of the false prophets, so they want to ignore all of them.

The day of the Lord, however, will fulfill all the visions except those of the false prophets. This day will come within their lifetimes (*in your days*). God's word is not for *many years* from now. The word spoken by the true prophet has set in motion the accomplishment of the visions from God.

Condemnation of False Prophets (13:1-23)

Ezekiel condemns those who prophesy falsely in God's name (verses 1-9), who mislead the people (verses 10-16), and who lead the people astray through magic and divination (verses 17-23).

Foxes Among the Ruins (13:1-9)

A true prophet must wait on a word from the Lord (see also Ezekiel 3:1-4; Jeremiah 23:9-32).

Foxes, in their natural habitat, can make a comfortable home for themselves in the ruins of a city. Calling the false prophets *jackals among ruins* shows that they have made themselves at home in Israel's troubles and are using it for their own benefit. They also are doing nothing to build up Israel's spiritual defenses (*a wall*) or to repair the damage which has been done to the covenant community because of sin.

The *register* (NRSV) or *records* (NIV) is a roll which lists people who are members of the political and religious community (see also Ezra 2).

A Whitewashed Wall (13:10-16)

False prophets are condemned because they seek to lull the people into a sense of well-being (*peace*). Ezekiel says that this sense of peace is a delusion. The people put up flimsy defenses (*a wall*) that give them a false sense of security, instead of relying on God. When the trials and testing of the day of the Lord come, these defenses will be no good. The people will recognize that the prophets were wrong, and the prophets will die (see also Jeremiah 28).

False Prophecy and Magic (13:17-23)

Ezekiel speaks out against Israelite women who practice magic and sorcery as prophecy. They discourage and victimize those who want to live a righteous life, and they encourage the wicked in their evil. They perhaps work their magic in God's name, dishonoring God and exploiting God's name for gain.

Some superstitious practices for warding off bad luck or disease include tying string, wool, cloth, or bark around certain parts of the body. Veils are used to cover the whole body in the magic power of the veil. This practice may be intended to give the sorcerer power over the lives and souls of the people wearing the veil.

Idolatry and Individual Responsibility (14:1-23)

The two oracles in chapter 14 deal with the consequences of letting one's life be taken over by idols (verses 1-11) and with each person's responsibility for his or her own salvation (verses 12-23).

Idols Lead to Alienation (14:1-11)

The central issue of this announcement of judgment is found in verses 7-8: No one may replace God with idols and still be part of God's people. Elders among the exiles come to Ezekiel seeking guidance from God but have no genuine commitment to God. They are perhaps combining idol worship with worship of God.

In Old Testament and New Testament thought, what is in one's heart determines one's whole life. The heart is the source of physical, intellectual, and emotional energy and of the will. The thoughts, hopes, fears, and values that come from the heart determine a person's character. We reflect this same belief when we speak of a person's heart being in the right place.

The right place for the hearts of the people of Israel is with God. This is true even of the sojourner, who was not born into the people of God but lives within the community of faith (see Judges 19:16-21; Leviticus 17:8-9).

The people of God live and thrive only when God's face looks on them with favor (see Numbers 6:25-26).

Verses 9-11: This part of the oracle explains an "if-then" situation. Its form is similar to a type of

Israelite law in which a hypothetical case is described and a judgment about it given (see Leviticus 17:3-5).

That prophets can be deceived by God may reflect the fact that God can test the people through false prophets (see Deuteronomy 13:1-5). The power to speak or to perform wonders is not proof that a prophet is true. The prophet and the prophecy must always point to God and increase people's faith in God.

Individual Responsibility (14:12-23)

Verses 12-21: When God's judgment comes each person's life will be examined individually. Only personal righteousness will save them.

Noah, Daniel (not the same person as in the Old Testament book of Daniel), and Job are known for their righteousness. Noah and Daniel are heroes from the days before Israel was a nation. Job is a non-Israelite (one of the *people of the east,* Job 1:3). That these men's lives are held up as examples shows that God is concerned for righteousness regardless of a person's nationality or religious heritage.

The principle of individual responsibility will be applied to the judgment of Jerusalem.

Verses 22-23: The unrighteous ones from Jerusalem who survive to go into exile will confirm to Ezekiel and the other exiles the justice of God's judgment.

Knowing that divine justice has been upheld will be a consolation to the people of Israel. Israel may take consolation and therefore hope from the fact that God has remained true to the covenant.

Parable of the Vine (15:1-8)

This announcement of judgment, which comes sometime between 592 and 587 B.C., is in the form of a parable and its interpretation.

The parable introduces a series of questions by which the value of the vine wood is to be judged. This vine is not valued for its fruit or its beauty (see for example, Isaiah 5:1-7; Psalm 80) but as fuel.

The interpretation of the parable (verses 6-8) shows that the vine wood is a metaphor for Jerusalem, and Jerusalem represents all Israel. Though Jerusalem has been burned and charred already (in the siege of 597 B.C.) the city will face yet another consuming fire of God's judgment (see verse 7).

§ § § § § § §

The Message of Ezekiel 12–15

This section opens with Ezekiel acting out for the exiles what they have already experienced in their journey from Jerusalem to Babylon. They must understand that they have not seen the last of such journeys. They must also be made to see what has happened and what will happen to Israel in the light of God's justice.

These chapters give examples of sin among the exiles and those in Jerusalem. Such examples build a case against Israel which makes sense according to the covenant that made them God's people. The basic terms of this covenant are stated in the Ten Commandments (see Exodus 20; Deuteronomy 5) and are expanded in other Scripture (see Exodus 21–23; Leviticus 26; Deuteronomy 28).

What does Ezekiel tell the exiles about God's intentions to be true to the covenant promises of judgment and of hope?

§ The vine—Israel—has produced sinful fruit and has abandoned the creator, the source of life for the vine.

§ Israel cannot rely on past promises or glory to save her now.

§ Israel cannot ignore or postpone the word of judgment.

§ § § § § § §

Ezekiel 16–19

Introduction to These Chapters

Ezekiel 16–19 shows us some of the creative ways in
which Ezekiel delivered his prophetic message. Chapters
16–17 are allegories. The oracles in chapter 18 use
Israelite legal forms and traditions. Chapter 19 is a
funeral lament.

Here is an outline of Ezekiel 16–19.

I. Allegory of Unfaithful Jerusalem (16:1-63)
   A. The unfaithful wife (16:1-43)
   B. The corrupt sister (16:44-58)
   C. Hope in the covenant (16:59-63)
II. Allegory of the Eagles (17:1-24)
III. The Soul That Sins Shall Die (18:1-32)
   A. Individual responsibility for sin (18:1-24)
   B. Turn, and live (18:25-32)
IV. A Lamentation for Israel's Leaders (19:1-14)
   A. The young lions (19:1-9)
   B. The withered vine (19:10-14)

Allegory of Unfaithful Jerusalem (16:1-63)

In chapter 16, Ezekiel tells the people of Israel a long
and intense tale about their own history. The story
narrates their beginnings as God's people and it tells
about how they slipped away from God. By telling their
history as a story, Ezekiel invites the people to stand
back from their own personal views. Through this
narrative, they can see how God looks at what has
happened in their lives.

The Unfaithful Wife (16:1-43)

Jerusalem (again as the representative for all Israel) is pictured as a helpless child who is abandoned by her parents. God takes pity on the child, saves her life, and adopts her through marriage. The wife, that is, Jerusalem, breaks her marriage vows to go after other gods and must then pay the price for her infidelity.

Verse 3: Jerusalem was not founded by the Israelites. (See 2 Samuel 5:6-10. See also the glossary for definitions of Canaanite, Amorite, and Hittite.)

Verses 4-5: Like many female babies in ancient times, the infant was not given customary care after birth and was abandoned to die.

Verse 8: The spreading of a shirt or robe is a commitment to marriage (see also Ruth 3:9). The marriage is solemnized in the covenant between God and Israel.

Verses 15-22: The wife—Israel—abuses the gifts given to her by God. She places her trust in the gifts (*beauty*) rather than in the giver.

Israel, the unfaithful wife, uses her wedding garments in order to build shrines in which pagan sexual rites take place. The *male idols* (NIV) or *male images* (NRSV) (verse 17) may be sexual symbols.

The bounty of the land (flour, oil, and honey) was God's gift to Israel. Now Israel offers these gifts to idols. She also offers the fruit of her body to idols (verses 20-21; see also Jeremiah 7:31), forgetting that her life depends on God.

Verses 23-29: A *lofty place* (NRSV) or *lofty shrine* (NIV) is perhaps a raised platform or altar that imitates the high places of Canaanite nature worship.

Playing *the whore* (NRSV) or engaging *in prostitution* (NIV) means that Israel made unwise political alliances with foreign nations and also worshiped the gods of these nations.

Verses 30-34: Israel is a different kind of harlot because she hires her lovers to come to her. Even in comparison to the shameful world of prostitution, Israel is unnatural (see also Jeremiah 2:23–3:5).

Verses 35-43: God announces judgment on Israel

because of her sins. The unfaithful wife's former lovers will be used to punish her. Israel will be left destitute as she was when God first took pity on her (verse 7).

Verse 42 introduces a note of future salvation which is taken up more fully in verses 60-63.

The Corrupt Sister (16:44-58)

This section expands on the theme of Jerusalem's pagan family. Though chosen for a special relationship with God, Jerusalem/Israel still shows her pagan roots and even outdoes her pagan relatives in sin. (See glossary for information on Samaria and Sodom.)

The only comfort Israel may take in her punishment is that she has made her sister's sins less by comparison. Even Israel's eventual restoration (verses 54-55) will comfort her wicked sisters and cause Israel to better appreciate her disgrace.

These verses explain how Israel is to understand and react to what has happened to her. In her shame, she is to be conscious of her guilt and failure (though some Israelites are too degenerate to even be ashamed, see Jeremiah 3:3). According to the prophet, the people's consciousness of shame and guilt can lead to eventual healing and regeneration.

Hope in the Covenant (16:59-63)

Although Israel broke the covenant with God that she swore to uphold, God will renew the covenant relationship. The past is not wiped out because Israel will remember her wickedness and be ashamed. But this remembrance will be the basis on which Israel may respond to God's love and forgiveness. This everlasting covenant will transform the people (see Jeremiah 31:31-34).

Allegory of the Eagles (17:1-24)

This riddle in the form of an allegory intends to teach the people of Israel that God's power, grace, and majesty are revealed in human history. The background of this allegory is the plots between King Zedekiah in Judah and the Egyptians to rebel against Babylonian control.

A *great eagle* refers to Nebuchadnezzar, the king of Babylon.

Lebanon refers to the high mountain ranges on Israel's northern borders where majestic cedar trees grew. The *top of the cedar* from Lebanon is a high or tall one, that is, one of the kings of the house of David.

The *topmost shoot* is King Jehoiachin of Judah who was taken to Babylon, *a land of trade* (NRSV) or *land of merchants* (NIV) by King Nebuchadnezzar. The *seed of your land* (NIV) or *seed from the land* (NRSV) refers to King Zedekiah of Judah who was given every opportunity to flourish by Nebuchadnezzar and by God, whose will it was for Judah to submit to the Babylonians. This seed grows into a healthy vine.

Another great eagle is Psammetichus II of Egypt, to whom Zedekiah turned for help against Babylon. Zedekiah's transplanted loyalties will cause the vine to die.

The *east wind* is Nebuchadnezzar.

Verses 11-18 explain the riddle. The oath and covenant between Zedekiah and Nebuchadnezzar are like a covenant between Zedekiah and God. The king, on behalf of Israel, made the covenant in the name of God (see 2 Chronicles 36:11-14). So Israel must face the consequences of this broken covenant (verses 19-21).

Verses 22-24: God now acts to bring a king of the royal line of David to God's holy mountain (the *high and lofty mountain*). This messianic king will grow into great fruitfulness and dominion. Even other nations (birds of every kind and *trees of the field*) will benefit from the *noble cedar* (NRSV) or *splendid cedar* (NIV) and will recognize the power of God.

The Soul That Sins Shall Die (18:1-32)

God disputes two beliefs held by the exiles—that their fathers are responsible for what has happened to them and that God is unjust to them.

Individual Responsibility for Sin (18:1-24)

Verses 1-4: The proverb in verse 2 may come from an interpretation of Exodus 20:5. Elsewhere in the Old Testament, however, the principle of individual responsibility for sin is upheld (see Jeremiah 31:27-30; Deuteronomy 24:16; 2 Kings 14:5-6). God replaces this proverb with another one: *The soul that sins shall die* (NIV) or *it is only the person who sins that shall die* (NRSV). This is both a warning and a sign of hope for life lived in righteousness.

In the Old Testament, a soul is a living being (see Genesis 2:7). The soul is the life force that includes both physical and spiritual qualities.

Verses 5-24: These verses use the example of three generations of righteous and sinful men (verses 5-9, 10-13, 14-18) to apply the principle laid down in verse 4. These test cases are similar in form to the laws in Leviticus 17–26.

The requirements for righteousness come from Exodus 20, Leviticus 15–26, and the book of Deuteronomy. The first rule forbids pagan worship (verse 6a).

The second rule forbids sexual misconduct and sexual uncleanness (verse 6b). Such misconduct may be a problem among the exiles because they are away from the traditional ties and restraints of home.

The third set of requirements deals with social issues (verses 7-8). The exiles are to care for one another and not exploit or ignore the poor.

Verses 19-24: This sums up the instructions given in the previous verses. An important part of God's nature is revealed in verse 23: God is for life in God's people, not for death. Neither is God indifferent to what happens to individual lives.

Turn and Live (18:25-32)

Verses 25-29: God demands that the people of Israel consider their own ways and sit honestly in judgment on themselves.

Verses 30-32: The people must actively turn away from and reject sin so that they may completely turn to God. This is a call to new life (see also Jeremiah 31:29-34).

A Lamentation for Israel's Leaders (19:1-14)

Laments are poems about grief and loss which are used in funeral services (see 2 Samuel 3:31-34) and in worship services (see Psalm 123; Lamentations 1-5).

The Young Lions (19:1-9)

Ezekiel laments two young kings of Judah who had short reigns and who were taken into captivity.

The mother *lioness* is Judah, in particular the house of David which ruled in Judah.

The first young lion (verses 2-4) is King Jehoahaz (609–608 B.C.), who was removed from power by the Egyptians and exiled in Egypt.

The second young lion is King Jehoiachin (597 B.C.) who became king during the Babylonian siege of Jerusalem and was exiled in Babylon.

The Withered Vine (19:10-14)

In this lament, Ezekiel speaks of Judah and the royal house of David as a vine (see also Ezekiel 15; Jeremiah 2:21). The vine enjoyed fruitfulness and health under God's blessing.

The strongest stem or branch may be King Zedekiah (597–587 B.C.). The *east wind* may be Babylonia. Though the east wind was harmful to the vine, forces within the vine itself (fire has gone out from its stem or main branch, verse 14) had a part in its downfall. Thus, the sins of the king (rebellion against Babylon) helped ruin his own house. This lament may have come after Zedekiah's defeat in 587 B.C.

§ § § § § § §

The Message of Ezekiel 16–19

Ezekiel tells the people of Israel that they must fully face and accept the depths to which they have fallen. The realities of sin and death are not to be avoided. Only in this hard and narrow way can they find life.

§ The people have disgraced themselves and God's holy name, and they must be ashamed.

§ Each person must examine his or her own life and make the decision to turn away from sin.

§ New hope and strength will not come from earthly rulers because they have been overwhelmed.

§ Israel's history as a people has been one of rebellion and sin. Only God's patience and mercy have kept the thread of salvation running through their long history of disobedience.

§ God's ultimate will is to save even those people who have sinned and have been unfaithful.

§ § § § § § §

PART SIX Ezekiel 20–24

Introduction to These Chapters

These chapters conclude the part of Ezekiel's prophecies which come for the most part between 593 and 587 B.C. (chapters 1–24). Chapters 20–23 tell the history of Israel's sins and of the consequences of these sins. Chapter 24 announces an end to this history of rebellion against God. This last chapter shows the depth of Ezekiel's commitment to his calling in a time of both personal and national tragedy.

Here is an outline of these chapters.

   I. A History of Rebellion (20:1-49)
  II. The Sword of the Lord (21:1-32)
 III. The Sins of Jerusalem (22:1-31)
 IV. The Allegory of Two Sisters (23:1-49)
  V. The Siege of Jerusalem (24:1-27)
     A. The pot of boiling flesh (24:1-14)
     B. The death of Ezekiel's wife (24:15-27)

A History of Rebellion (20:1-49)

Through repeated disobedience and rebellion against God the people of Israel have proved that they do not merit God's graciousness to them (verses 1-32, 45-49). Only for the sake of God's sacred name and honor will they be restored (verses 33-44).

Verses 1-32. On August 14, 591 B.C. certain elders come to question God through Ezekiel. Ezekiel answers them with a history of their people. This history is one in which Israel continually rejected God's instructions. Three generations of Israelites and three instances of rebellion are named.

Verses 5-9: Through God's self-revelation to Israel (see Exodus 6:1-9), the people were promised freedom and a bountiful land to call home. But even in their slavery, the people rebelled and followed idols. God withheld punishment, however, so that the destruction of the people called by God's name would not bring disgrace to God's name among other nations.

Verses 10-17: In the wilderness God gave Israel the Law (see Exodus 20) which contains both sacred and civil regulations. God also gave Israel the sabbath as a sign of the covenant relationship (see Exodus 31:13-17). Yet Israel rejected these life-giving gifts.

Verses 18-26: Though given a chance to be faithful participants in the covenant, the children of the Exodus generation also disobeyed.

Israel had been warned about the possibility of exile (Deuteronomy 4:25-31) but continued to worship idols.

Within the Law itself are the possibilities for life and for death (verses 25-26). The perversion of God's law will lead to darkness and death instead of to light and life (see also Ezekiel 14:9, Romans 5:20; 7:7-12).

Verse 26 refers to human sacrifice which was also practiced by some Canaanite cults. During the time of King Ahaz and King Manasseh, God's instructions to consecrate first-born sons (see Exodus 22:29) were taken literally (see 2 Kings 16:3).

Verses 27-31: The present generation of Israelites is following in their fathers' footsteps. Their divided loyalties have alienated them from God.

Verses 33-39: The people of Israel will be led out of exile only to face God as both king and judge. The *wilderness of the peoples* (NRSV) or *desert of the nations* (NIV) may refer to the Syrian wilderness or it may refer to a place of judgment which recalls Israel's former judgment in the wilderness of Sinai (see Numbers 14:13-25).

To *pass under my rod* (NIV) or *staff* (NRSV) reflects the practice of a shepherd who has each animal in his flock walk under his outstretched staff so that he may count them and separate out those he does not want to keep.

Verses 40-44: The exiles will be led in a new Exodus to Zion, God's holy mountain. There their worship will be pure and they will be restored to a right relationship with God. God's holiness and power will be evident to Israel and to the world.

Verses 45-49: The fire of God's judgment will consume Judah (the *south*). God's name will be upheld in the sight of the world (*all flesh* [NRSV] or *everyone* [NIV]) because they will know that God has punished Israel.

Ezekiel tells God that his listeners are accusing him of telling stories which they cannot understand and which they ignore.

The Sword of the Lord (21:1-32)

Ezekiel demonstrates and tells of the coming destruction.

Verses 1-7: In Babylonia Ezekiel preaches against the sanctuaries of idol worship in Israel. In front of the exiles he sighs and grieves because of the warfare which is coming to the land of Judah. When the exiles hear of Judah's fate (see Ezekiel 33:21) they also will grieve and be afraid.

Verses 8-17: In delivering this announcement of judgment, Ezekiel performs five symbolic actions. He cries and wails and strikes his thigh as people do in mourning. He claps his hands to signal the beginning of judgment. He brings his sword down three times and then cuts with it to the right and left as symbols of the complete destruction that is coming.

This punishment is coming because the people

despised the *rod* (NRSV) or *sceptor* (NIV) of God's discipline and went after idols.

Verses 18-24: In 589 B.C. Judah and Ammon were part of an alliance in rebellion against Babylon. The *sword* of the king of Babylon will act as God's sword of judgment. Nebuchadnezzar will have to decide how to attack Judah and Ammon. Ezekiel is to prepare a signpost which will symbolically guide Nebuchadnezzar in his attack.

Nebuchadnezzar uses divination to plan his campaign. Arrows are marked with choices of action and then are drawn out of a quiver at random. *Teraphim* (NRSV) are household *idols* (NIV). The liver of a sheep is examined for favorable signs.

Verse 22 describes the siege of Jerusalem. The people of Jerusalem will not believe that Nebuchadnezzar will attack them, even though they break the oaths of allegiance they have sworn to him. The Babylonian king is God's prosecutor and executioner against Jerusalem (verse 23).

Verses 25-27: The *prince* is King Zedekiah. He will lose the symbols of his office (*crown* and *turban*) and will be brought low (see also Jeremiah 21:3-7). Jerusalem, the Temple, and the power of Israel's ruling family will be left in ruins. No evidence of Israel's greatness will remain until God restores Israel under a rightful ruler (see Ezekiel 37; Genesis 49:10).

Verses 28-32: The Ammonites are the *wicked* who rebel against Babylon. They, no less than Israel, will be punished by the Babylonians.

The Sins of Jerusalem (22:1-31)

In three oracles Ezekiel tells of the crimes and sins of the people in Jerusalem.

Verses 1-16: Jerusalem is condemned because of the conduct of the people who live there. The people are guilty of idolatry, adultery, fornication, injustice, violence, slander, extortion, and contempt for what is holy (compare these sins with the regulations in Leviticus 17–26). All this wickedness will not be able to withstand the day of the Lord's punishment.

Verses 17-22: Ezekiel describes God's punishment of the wicked people in Jerusalem as being like a smelter in which metal is heated. Though the people were once valuable, as the metals of verse 18 are valuable, they are now only as the impurities which come from the metal. Jerusalem is the furnace in which they will feel the refining fire of judgment.

Verses 23-31: The sins of the people have made the land unclean. The land will not be blessed with life-giving, cleansing rain on the day of God's *wrath* (NIV) or *indignation* (NRSV). This is because all classes of people in Judah have abandoned their responsibilities as members of the community of faith. The princes, instead of protecting and leading the people, have preyed on them. The priests do not uphold their duties in regard to the law or worship. Prophets prophesy out of their own minds and mislead the people. The common people victimize one another instead of caring for one another.

The Allegory of Two Sisters (23:1-49)

This is another story about Israel's sins of the past and the present. In the story two sisters represent the two kingdoms of Israel. Oholah represents Samaria, which was the capital of the Northern Kingdom of Israel. Oholibah represents Jerusalem, which is the capital of the Southern Kingdom of Judah.

Verses 1-4: The sins of these sisters began when they and their people were slaves in Egypt (see 20:8).

Verses 5-10: The Northern Kingdom of Israel was at times dominated politically by Assyria and was completely taken over in 722 B.C. Israel also took up the worship of foreign gods. Because she broke her covenant vows of loyalty to God, her former *lovers* were allowed to destroy her (see also Hosea 8:1–9:3).

Verses 11-21: Judah does not learn from her sister's downfall but rather follows in her footsteps (see also Jeremiah 3:6-10). Judah made alliances with Assyria, Babylonia (*the Chaldeans*), and Egypt. She took up the worship of their gods, which included sexual acts performed as fertility rites.

Verses 22-35: The power and virility of Judah's former lovers which once attracted her to them will now be used against her.

Cutting off the nose and ears of adult captives was a Mesopotamian custom of war.

The exposure the people of Judah will suffer as captives of war will expose or reveal to them the harlotry of their idol worship.

The *cup* is a symbol of destiny and Judah must drink the same cup of God's wrath as did her sister.

Judah forgot God and remembered only her idols, therefore she must bear the consequences that were spelled out in the marriage/covenant agreement.

Verses 36-49: The punishment of adultery is stoning (see Leviticus 20:10). The sisters commit adultery through human sacrifice and pagan worship, even in the Temple and on the sabbath. Therefore, they must bear the penalty for their sins.

The Siege of Jerusalem (24:1-27)

The destruction of Jerusalem (verses 1-14) will leave the exiles numb with grief just as Ezekiel is after his wife's death (verses 15-27).

The Pot of Boiling Flesh (24:1-14)

On January 15, 588 B.C., Babylonian forces laid siege to Jerusalem. Ezekiel tells the exiles an allegory about the meaning of this day and its eventual outcome. Jerusalem is again compared to a pot in which its citizens will be boiled. The logs under the pot are the siege equipment used by the attackers: ladders, battering rams, catapults, and archery towers. The Babylonians will light the fires that will, in the summer of 587 B.C., finally burn the city.

The people of Jerusalem are guilty of shedding innocent blood, both in ritual sacrifices (see 20:26) and in crimes of violence (see 22:35). Bloodguilt must be punished (see also Deuteronomy 19:9-10; Jeremiah 26:15), especially since the people do not even show an awareness of their crimes by trying to cover them up.

A second theme in the allegory is that of the rust of corruption being cleansed from the city. The underlying wickedness and guilt that has corroded the very structure of the covenant community must be burned away.

The Death of Ezekiel's Wife (24:15-27)

During the time close to the end of the siege of Jerusalem (perhaps during the early summer of 587 B.C.) God tells Ezekiel that his wife (*the delight of your eyes*) is going to die soon. Ezekiel's reaction to this personal tragedy is going to show the exiles what they will go through when Jerusalem is destroyed.

Ezekiel will grieve inwardly but must give no outward sign of his great loss. In mourning rituals a person would let his or her hair hang loose and cover it with dirt or ashes. The mourner would go barefoot and would perhaps cover his or her head down to the upper lip. Friends would bring bread to help call the mourner back to the world of the living. All these expressions of comfort and ways of coping with loss are denied to Ezekiel.

The exiles will be numb with grief and shock when they know that the Temple has been destroyed and their loved ones in Jerusalem killed. Like Ezekiel, they will be unable to express the depth of their tragedy.

Ezekiel will be unable to speak for a time before they know that Jerusalem has fallen. When a messenger arrives with the news, Ezekiel will again be able to talk (see Ezekiel 33:21-22). All of these things will be a sign, that is, a confirmation and a revelation of God's power.

§ § § § § § §

The Message of Ezekiel 20–24

In early 588 B.C., at the beginning of the end for the city of Jerusalem, Ezekiel must also bear the loss of his beloved wife. He remains true to his calling, however, and submits his grief to the purposes of God's word. What does Ezekiel's life as a man and a prophet tell us?

§ The prophet is not exempt from pain. He is a messenger and a witness who suffers along with his people under God's judgment.

§ Because the prophet also bears God's judgment, his life becomes a symbol of hope. That God speaks through a witness who is himself under judgment shows that God has not abandoned the people called by God's name.

§ God's servants must have the capacity and willingness to listen, to speak, to care, to feel, and to suffer for the sake of God's word.

§ § § § § § §

Ezekiel 25–28

Introduction to These Chapters

Ezekiel 25–32 is a collection of announcements of judgment against foreign nations. The nations are condemned because they have been involved in Israel's rebellion against Babylon or because they have taken advantage of Judah's desperate situation for their own gain. Most of these oracles are from around 587 B.C. Here is an outline of these chapters.

I. Ammon, Moab, Edom, and Philistia (25:1-17)
   A. Against Ammon (25:1-7)
   B. Against Moab (25:8-11)
   C. Against Edom (25:12-14)
   D. Against the Philistines (25:15-17)
II. Against Tyre (26:1–28:19)
   A. Tyre will be given to Babylon (26:1-21)
   B. Lamentation over Tyre (27:1-36)
   C. Judgment and hope (28:1-19)
   D. The end of a proud king (28:1-10)
   E. Lament for the King of Tyre (29:11-19)
III. Judgment Against Sidon (28:20-26)

Ammon, Moab, Edom, and Philistia (25:1-17)

Though the people of these countries may not actually hear Ezekiel speak words against them, the power of God's judgment is set in motion by the prophetic word.

Against Ammon (25:1-7)

Ammon was an old rival of Israel (see also Judges 10:6-9) who rejoiced over Israel's defeat. Ammon will be punished because of this (see also Jeremiah 49:1-6).

The *people of the East* are nomadic, cattle-breeding tribes from the desert and steppe region east of the cultivated areas along the eastern side of the Jordan River.

Against Moab (25:8-11)

Edom, Moab, Ammon, Tyre, and Sidon all plotted with Judah to rebel against Babylon (see Jeremiah 27:1-11). There was also a long history of struggle between Moab and Israel (see Judges 3:12-30). The people of Moab see Jerusalem's destruction and misinterpret what it means. They believe that this makes Judah like any other nation. Their own judgment, however, will reveal to them the power of the God of Judah.

Against Edom (25:12-14)

Edom and Israel were longstanding rivals (see 1 Kings 11:14-25) even though the two were supposed to be brothers (see Deuteronomy 23:7-8). By 587 B.C., people from Edom had taken over parts of southern Judah because of the occupation of their own territory by peoples of the east.

Against the Philistines (25:15-17)

The Philistines also had longstanding conflicts with Israel. They perhaps tried to take advantage of Judah's weakened condition after 587 B.C. though acts of political or military vengeance.

Against Tyre (26:1–28:19)

Ezekiel speaks more oracles against Tyre and Egypt than against the other nations. This is because they were more important politically, militarily, and economically than these other nations. They were great obstacles to

Nebuchadnezzar's success as God's instrument of judgment.

Tyre's strength and wealth came in large part from her geographical position and her success in trade. Tyre lay one-half mile off the shore of Palestine in the Mediterranean Sea on a rocky island. The city had two harbors.

Tyre Will Be Given to Babylon (26:1-21)

After Jerusalem's destruction in 587 B.C. Tyre saw a chance to increase her strength in the region perhaps by controlling more of the overland trade routes. However, in 586 B.C. Nebuchadnezzar laid siege to the city of Tyre. This siege lasted thirteen years and ended with a negotiated settlement in which the people of Tyre became subjects of Babylon.

Verse 1: Some manuscripts say *twelfth year* instead of *eleventh year.* The twelfth year of the reign of King Jehoiachin is early 586 B.C.

Verse 6: Its *daughter-towns* (NRSV) are Tyre's *settlements* (NIV) on the mainland coast.

Verses 7-14: The rich, comfortable life of Tyre's merchants will be overwhelmed by the military might of Babylon. Tyre will become a place where only fishermen spread their nets.

Verses 15-21: The *princes of the sea* (NRSV) or *coast* (NIV) are perhaps rulers of other commercial cities who trade with Tyre. These princes will go through a mourning ritual for Tyre and voice a lament over her death. That one so mighty could fall is cause for grief and fear.

The *ocean depths* (NIV) or *deep* (NRSV) and the vast *waters* are the primeval deep on which God set limits at creation (see Genesis 1:2-8) and which broke loose at the Flood (see Genesis 7:11). These waters are thought to be like an underground ocean and are associated with the depths of the earth. In these depths is the Pit or Sheol, which is the land of the dead.

The *people of long ago* are like the dead of long ago (see Lamentations 3:6). They live in a dusty, dry world without peace or joy. The powers of death will carry away mighty Tyre.

Lamentation Over Tyre (27:1-36)

Ezekiel is to speak a funeral lament over the fall of the city of Tyre. In such a lament, the earthly beauty and power of the deceased (verses 3-25) and their downfall and death (verses 26-36) are described. Because Tyre was prosperous and well known in international trade, the city is spoken of as a well-built merchant ship.

Verses 3-9: The ship that represents Tyre is built of the finest materials from many lands and is handled by a skilled crew. (See the glossary for place name identifications.)

Verses 10-25: This is a list of Tyre's military allies and trading partners. The list shows the extent of Tyre's trading relationships and the wealth of goods in which she traded. The merchants of Tyre truly *satisfied many* and did *enrich the kings of the earth* (see verse 33).

Cassia and *calamus* (NIV) or *sweet cane* (NRSV) (verse 19) are spices, perhaps cinnamon and sweet cane.

Verses 25-36: The ship goes out onto the high seas to conduct her business as usual and is wrecked by the *east wind* (King Nebuchadnezzar).

The ruin of such a powerful ship as Tyre brings grief and fear to the seamen, merchants, and other inhabitants of the coastlands. They go through mourning rituals as they would for a loved one (verses 30-31). They wail and sing a funeral lament (verses 32-36). If such a tragedy could happen to a great city then it could also happen to them.

A *hiss* (verse 36) is a sign of astonishment or contempt. Or it may be an act to scare off demons of destruction (see also Jeremiah 18:13-17).

Judgment and Hope (28:1-19)

Ezekiel announces judgment for Tyre (verses 1-10, 11-19) and Sidon (verses 20-23), and restoration for Israel (verses 24-26).

The End of a Proud King (28:1-10)

The prince or king of Tyre is addressed in this oracle as the representative of the city of Tyre in its military and economic self-confidence. The announcement of judgment focuses on two qualities of the king: his proud heart and his claim to be a god.

In the ancient Near East it was not unusual for pagan kings to be considered as god incarnate and as the one who could guarantee their peoples' salvation. Such a king would indeed be looked upon as one *wise as a god* (NIV) or *with the mind of a god* (NRSV).

Wisdom was not seen as just an intellectual ability. Wisdom was also viewed as a means of mastering life. This particular king's wisdom had reaped him (and his city) riches and power through trade. The gift of wisdom, the accumulation of wealth, and the seeming invulnerability of a god led to a fatal pride of the heart. The king will now face the consequences for having overstepped the bounds between what is rightfully his and what is God's.

The most terrible or ruthless *of the nations* is Babylon.

Daniel is probably the wise man from the time of the patriarchs also spoken of in Ezekiel 14:12-20.

The *heart of the seas* may refer to Tyre's location on an island in the Mediterranean Sea.

Lament for the King of Tyre (28:11-19)

This is an announcement of judgment in the form of a lament. The king's past glory is described and the reasons given for his dreadful end.

The king is addressed as a man of Eden who lived in special favor and relationship with God. The man was blessed with beauty and wisdom which he used to gain trade and splendor. The corruption of these gifts led to violence, pride, and greed. Because of these sins, the king is cast out of favor with God. He will disappear from the earth and will be an object of fear and grief to other people (see also Ezekiel 27).

A *signet of perfection* (NRSV) or *model of perfection* (NIV) may refer to a signet ring which is a symbol of authority.

The mountain *of God* may be the holy mountain (see Psalm 48:1) or the mount of assembly (see Isaiah 14:13).

The stones of fire may be stars or other heavenly beings.

Judgment Against Sidon (28:20-23)

Sidon had been an ally of Jerusalem against Babylon (see Jeremiah 27:3). No specific charges are spoken against the city within this oracle. Rather, her fall will be a testimony to the power of God. God's glory and holiness will be revealed to Sidon and to other nations.

Restoration for Israel (28:24-26)

These verses tell how the punishment of Israel's pagan neighbors will affect the people of Israel.

Verse 24: Israel will no longer be wounded by these other nations nor looked down upon by them.

Verses 25-26: These verses are a conclusion for the collection of oracles against foreign nations in chapters 25–28. God will bring the exiles home to live once again under the covenant in the Promised Land. This action will show God's holiness to the nations.

§ § § § § § §

The Message of Ezekiel 25–28

These oracles against the nations are related to the political and military realities that the people of Israel faced in their life as a nation. God's people live in history, not apart from it. These oracles point to a larger perspective than just particular historical circumstances, however. They point to God as the Lord of all peoples who commands the powers of life and death.

§ God judges and rules the destiny of humankind.

§ Human pride and earthly power and might must always yield to God's power and will.

§ God gives human beings wonderful gifts (for example, the wisdom to master life). But the gifts must always be used according to God's laws, and the giver must always be acknowledged as the ultimate source of power.

§ God's nature and will are revealed to Israel and to other nations through the prophetic word.

§ In their punishment and in their restoration the people of Israel will be a witness to God's power and will come to a new knowledge of God.

§ § § § § § §

Ezekiel 29–32

Introduction to These Chapters

Chapters 29–32 are a series of announcements of judgment against Egypt. Ezekiel strongly condemns Egypt because of Egypt's pride, and because Egypt encouraged Israel to rebel against Babylon. Here is an outline of these chapters.

I. Prophecy Against the Pharaoh (29:1-21)
II. The Day of the Lord (30:1-26)
III. Allegory of Pharaoh as a Cedar Tree (31:1-18)
IV. Lamentations over Egypt (32:1-32)
   A. Lament over Pharaoh (32:1-16)
   B. Egypt sent down to the pit (32:17-32)

Prophecy Against the Pharaoh (29:1-21)

Both Ezekiel and Jeremiah warned Israel not to rely on Egypt as an ally against Babylon (see Jeremiah 37:6-10, 46:1-26). Both of these prophets recognized Babylon as God's sword of punishment to which Israel must eventually yield.

Verses 1-16: On January 7, 587 B.C., word comes to Ezekiel to prophesy against Pharaoh Hophra of Egypt. Ezekiel addresses the Pharaoh as *a great monster* (NIV) or *dragon* (NRSV). This dragon is similar to the Egyptian images of their pharaoh as a crocodile. The dragon is also similar to the monster of chaos that opposes the creative powers of God (see also Psalm 74:12-17).

This proud and powerful dragon claims the Nile as his

own creation. But the king/dragon and his armies (*the fish of your streams* [NIV] or *channels* [NRSV]) will be destroyed by the true creator of all things.

Egypt is also condemned for being an unreliable ally to Israel. Israel leaned on Egyptian military might against the Babylonians rather than leaning on God's will.

After forty years of punishment Egypt will be restored (also Judah, see Ezekiel 4:6). The punishment and restoration will set things to right in Egypt. Egypt will no longer be a proud and mighty nation, nor will it again tempt Israel to put false trust in its power. And, as in all of God's actions, knowledge of God in Egypt and in Israel will increase.

Verses 17-20: This is the latest dated oracle in Ezekiel, April 26, 571 B.C. Nebuchadnezzar did not receive the appropriate amount of spoils for his long years of labor in the siege of Tyre. After thirteen years of warfare the city probably had few riches to offer the Babylonians. Nebuchadnezzar is to be compensated for this with riches from Egypt.

In 568–567 B.C. Babylonian forces moved against Egypt and proved their military superiority. Egypt did not threaten Babylon again and the two nations lived in peace until both were overtaken by the Persians.

Verse 21: The dawn of Israel's restoration will come on God's day of destruction for Israel's enemies.

The *horn* is a symbol of strength that refers to Israel's coming deliverance.

Ezekiel's lips will be opened in the sense that his message will have fresh authority and truth to his listeners. The punishment of Egypt will confirm Ezekiel's words to the exiles and will give them a new revelation of God.

The Day of the Lord (30:1-26)

In poetry (verses 1-19) and in prose (verses 20-26) Ezekiel tells what the day of the Lord will mean for Egypt. Verses 1-19 are not dated but probably come from a time before Nebuchadnezzar's campaign against Egypt in 568/567 B.C. Verses 20-26 are dated April 29, 587 B.C.

Verses 1-9: The *day of the* LORD is God's day of judgment (see also Ezekiel 7; Amos 5:18; Jeremiah 30:7). God's power will move on an international scale against Egypt and her allies.

Ethiopia (also called Cush) will hear of Egypt's downfall and know that her fate will be the same.

Verses 10-12: God's power will come against Egypt through Nebuchadnezzar and through the drying up of the Nile which is the source of life for Egypt. The spoken word of the Lord begins the process of fulfilling the prophecy.

Verses 13-19: One by one the cities of Egypt fall. These acts of judgment testify to God's overwhelming power. These events also are clear evidence of God's determination that all people will come to know God as Lord of creation and of history.

Verses 20-26: In the spring of 588 B.C., the Egyptians attacked the Babylonian forces that surrounded Jerusalem. The Babylonians withdrew from Jerusalem for a time and drove off the Egyptians. They returned to Jerusalem and continued their siege. In the spring of 587 B.C. Jerusalem was about to be overrun and destroyed. Though the Egyptians had done Jerusalem's cause no good, they had not been completely broken themselves.

Ezekiel announces that they will not get off so lightly. The arms symbolize power.

Allegory of Pharaoh as a Cedar Tree (31:1-18)

Again in both poetry and prose Ezekiel tells of Egypt's fate. This oracle is dated June 21, 587 B.C.

Verses 2-9: Pharaoh is spoken of as a giant cedar tree. Its branches are in heaven and its roots are nourished by the waters of the primeval deep under the earth. The waters of the deep nourish the tree so that it is greater and more beautiful than other trees.

This tree offers protection to birds and beasts, that is,

to other nations. In splendor it surpasses even the trees of Eden in its God-given beauty. This symbolism shows Egypt's power and wealth in relation to her neighbors.

Verses 10-14: All beauty and power come from God, but the tree does not recognize this. A proud and arrogant heart leads to its downfall.

The ruler (NIV) or *prince* (NRSV) *of the nations* is Nebuchadnezzar.

The purpose of Egypt's destruction is given in verse 14. Egypt's fate is to be a sign that no one may seek to rival God and get away with it (compare Genesis 3).

Verses 15-18: The great tree (Pharaoh and his armies) will go to the land of the dead. The chaotic waters of the deep and other nations will mourn its passing. There will be disruptions in nature and in national life.

In death the once-great tree will lie among common trees (other nations) who have died a dishonorable or violent death. Its powerlessness before God will be made plain and its claims to greatness shown to be false.

Lament over Pharaoh (32:1-16)

This lament which announces judgment on Egypt is dated March 3, 585 B.C.

Again Pharaoh is compared to a dragon (see also Ezekiel 29:1-5). Though he thinks of himself as a lion, which is a symbol of royal power, he is in fact only like a sea monster. This dragon troubles the political and military waters around Judah.

Even after the fall of Jerusalem in August 587 B.C. Egypt tempted Israel to disobey God's will. In 582/581 B.C. a group of people from Judah fled to Egypt despite Jeremiah's warnings that it was God's will for them to stay in Judah (see Jeremiah 42:7–43:13).

The heavens will reflect Egypt's day of doom. This day is like the day of the Lord when everyone who opposes God is overcome (see also Isaiah 13:9-10; Joel 2:1-2).

The only consolation offered is that the waters of

Egypt will one day be restored, and that through all this God will be made known to the peoples of the earth.

This song of Egypt's destruction will be taken up by women of other nations as well. They will chant as professional mourning women do in funeral rituals (see also Jeremiah 9:17-21).

Egypt Sent Down to the Pit (32:17-32)

Ezekiel receives this word from God to wail over Egypt on April 27, 586 B.C. The prophetic word sets in motion the accomplishment of God's will. Thus, the word as well as the swords of the Babylonian warriors will *send them down* (NRSV) to death or *consign to the earth below* (NIV). Wailing and shrill cries are part of rituals of mourning for the dead.

The circumstances of life and the treatment of a dead body affect the fate of a person in the land of the dead. Those who are uncircumcised, who are executed, or who die under dishonorable circumstances and are not properly buried go to a place for the unclean. The righteous dead who receive an honorable burial go to a separate place in the land of the dead.

The *mighty leaders* (NIV) or *chiefs* (NRSV) may be the mighty men of verse 27 who lie in a place of honor.

Egypt will join other nations that have faced God's judgment. Each of these nations *spread terror in the land of the living* through their military might, and they each faced divine retribution.

The *princes of the north* are rulers in Phoenicia and Syria (see glossary for identifications of the other nations).

The warriors who have fallen are heroes of the past who lie in honor in Sheol. Though they, too, spread terror in life, it was perhaps not the ungodly terror spread by those who are condemned by God.

Pharaoh's bitter consolation will be that he is not alone in a shameful death. Other great earthly powers have gone before him into the Pit.

§ § § § § § §

The Message of Ezekiel 29–32

Ezekiel's prophecies serve more than one purpose within his ministry. The laments and oracles against Egypt show these different purposes. The prophetic word teaches new knowledge of God and of God's ways, reproaches wrongdoers, tells God's intentions for the future, and acts to begin the process of accomplishing God's will. What do these oracles and laments teach Israel and Egypt?

§ There is no earthly power to which Israel may look to avoid dealing with God.

§ There is no avenue of escape for anyone from God's will.

§ All peoples are under the constraints of divine justice.

§ Divine justice follows a person into the world after death.

§ § § § § § §

Ezekiel 33–39

Introduction to These Chapters

Chapters 33–39 in the book of Ezekiel come from the period of time after the destruction of Jerusalem in 587 B.C. The material in these chapters speaks of the siege of Jerusalem and of the Exile. These prophecies also look forward to the restoration of the homeland of Israel's people.

Here is an outline of these chapters.

Responsibility of Prophet and People (33:1-33)

Chapter 33 explains the standards of divine justice for both prophet and people. Punishment results if these standards are not adhered to.

Responsibility and Judgment (33:1-20)

Verses 1-9: God compares Ezekiel's duties as a prophet to those of a city watchman in time of war. If a city is threatened by an enemy, then one man is chosen to stand watch and blow a trumpet as a warning signal at the approach of the enemy. In this case, God is the enemy who is coming, and Ezekiel must warn Israel of the consequences of wickedness.

The watchman who does not do his duty will have the blood of the unwarned victims on his head. This is called bloodguiltiness, which is guilt brought on by bloodshed. Bloodguilt comes from unintentional or indirect bloodshed as well as from murder or negligence.

Verses 10-20: Ezekiel must confront two false beliefs. One is that there is no way to life for the people (verse 10), and the other is that God is unjust (verse 17).

The people recognize that their sins have led them to the point of death and they confess this. Now, however, they must meet God in the message of the prophet and make a decision for life or death. God's will is to redeem the people of Israel but they must turn away from evil.

This turning away is not just in attitudes or beliefs. Turning away from sin and turning toward righteousness involve being in right relationship to God and to other people. This relationship is shown by practicing justice and righteousness.

The requirements given in verse 15 promote healthy and caring relationships within the community of faith (see also Ezekiel 20:11). A pledge is a piece of personal property that a borrower gives to a lender to guarantee that a debt will be paid.

Jerusalem Has Fallen (33:21-22)

An eyewitness to Jerusalem's disaster brings the news to Ezekiel on January 19, 586 B.C. (Some Hebrew manuscripts read the *twelfth year* (585 B.C.) and others read the *eleventh year* (586 B.C.)

These verses pick up the sequence of events that was broken off in Ezekiel 24:25-27. Ezekiel's renewed call to be a watchman for Israel opens the final section of his work. This section looks toward the restoration and return of the people of Israel to the Promised Land.

Possessiveness and Sin (33:23-29)

Some people in Judah who have survived the battles with the Babylonians and were not taken into exile set about claiming the property of the exiles in Babylon. They claim for themselves the promise of the land that was given to Abraham. In this time of judgment they seek refuge in promises of the past, but they continue in their sin.

Babylonian occupation forces were in the land, and the people left in Judah were struggling to make sense out of what had happened to them (see also Lamentations 1–5; 2 Kings 23; Jeremiah 40–41).

The Exiles Do Not Hear (33:30-33)

Ezekiel fulfills his call as a watchman. The exiles listen, even seeking out the prophetic message. They accept the words of love but refuse to accept the words of judgment for themselves. Like those Israelites still in Judah, the exiles' hearts are preoccupied with greed (*gain*).

When God's judgment comes, however, the exiles will know that they were fairly warned by Ezekiel.

The Shepherds and Sheep of Israel (34:1-31)

Chapter 34 applies the issue of responsibility to Israel's rulers (*shepherds*) and to individual members of the covenant community (*sheep*).

God Will Be Israel's Shepherd (34:1-16)

The duties of a real shepherd, which the exiles certainly know, are applied to the rulers of the people of Israel. A shepherd could rightfully use the resources of the flock to feed and clothe himself. In return, however, the shepherd must care for the flock. Israel's leaders have special responsibilities toward the people, and they are condemned for neglecting these responsibilities and for taking advantage of people (see also Ezekiel 22:23-31).

God will rescue the scattered flock and become the true leader of Israel. The people will be led back into their land and will live in peace and fruitfulness under God's care. In this way justice and righteousness will be established in the flock once again.

God Is Both Shepherd and Judge (34:17-31)

Verses 17-24: There is oppression even within the community of faith. Because of this, the present leaders will be replaced by a *prince* from the royal line of David who will care for and lead the people. Proper relationships will be reestablished between the people and God and between the people and their prince (verse 24).

Verses 25-31: A new harmony between God, God's people, and nature is made possible through a new covenant. This *covenant of peace* will bring a profound state of well-being to people and land. Fear and slavery will be replaced by security and prosperity. This well-being comes from a new knowledge of their identification as God's people. In a sense, the people of Israel will be created anew as they were when they were first called by God's name (compare Jeremiah 31:31-34).

Oracle Against Mount Seir (35:1-15)

In these announcements of judgment (verses 1-4, 5-9, 10-15) Mount Seir stands for the nation of Edom. Edom is condemned for crimes against Israel (compare the oracle against Edom in Ezekiel 25:12-14, also compare Jeremiah 49:17-22; Obadiah 9-14). The prophecies of Edom's destruction serve to highlight the prophecies of Israel's restoration which follow in chapter 36.

Fulfillment and Restoration (36:1-38)

Ezekiel addresses the mountains, or highlands, of Israel as respresentatives of all Israel.

Prophecy to the Mountains of Israel (36:1-15)

These verses are a collection of short messages framed by the phrases *Thus says the Lord God* (NRSV) or *This is what the Sovereign Lord says* (NIV) and *therefore,* which are familiar parts of prophetic speech.

The crimes of the nations are similar to those Ezekiel has spoken of before—having a contemptuous attitude toward Israel and taking over Israelite territory.

In contrast to the nations, Israel will be blessed. Both the land and the people will be fruitful as in former times (see Genesis 1:22; Deuteronomy 28:11). The *inheritance of the house of Israel* includes the territory and people of Israel and of Judah.

The mountains will no longer be the sites of pagan worship or human sacrifice (verses 12-14). There will no longer be alienation between the people and the land. Israel will be a land of honor and not a land of disgrace.

For the Sake of God's Name (36:16-32)

Israel has a long history of sin (verses 16-21) but will be saved for the sake of God's holy name (verses 22-32).

God punished the people of Israel and sent them into exile for their sins of idolatry and of violence to one another. Yet, in exile, they were a source of dishonor to God because they were a people called by God's name. Other peoples looked down on God's power because God's people were powerless.

In biblical thought, the name of a person or of God is more than an identification. A name is also an expression of the character of the one named. God's honor and holiness are revealed in God's name.

The people of Israel are called by God's name. Therefore, they must also reflect the divine honor and holiness. Salvation will come to Israel because God will act to protect God's name.

The exiles will come home, and they will be purified in a cleansing ritual (see also Exodus 30:17-21; Numbers 19:17-19). The ritual described in verse 25 influenced baptismal rituals in the Jewish Qumran community (which produced the Dead Sea Scrolls) and in the Christian church.

The people of Israel will be created anew from the inside out. Their rebellious hearts of stone will be replaced by hearts devoted to God's will. A new spirit will bring a new disposition inclined toward God (see also the promises of Jeremiah 31:31-34). Earth and people will be renewed. In all of this Israel must remember her past sins and focus her new life on God and God's goodness.

God Will Be Revealed (36:33-38)

God's presence as creator and redeemer will be revealed even to the nations. In Old Testament belief, salvation is not only a state of inward righteousness but is also manifested by abundance and prosperity in the lives of God's people.

In verse 37 the word translated *people* (NIV) or *population* (NRSV) comes from the Hebrew word *adam* which means human being. This word can mean an individual or humankind as a whole. God's people will multiply like a *flock for sacrifices* or *offerings* as evidence of the power of God.

The Valley of Dry Bones (37:1-28)

This vision probably comes from a time after the fall of Jerusalem in 587 B.C. but before the exiles fully understand that they may yet live despite their sin (see Ezekiel 33:10).

Verses 1-14: The very dry bones show that death has long since triumphed in the visionary valley to which

Ezekiel is taken. The dead lie here in disgrace because they did not receive a proper burial.

Ezekiel speaks two words to the bones. The first word gives the bones human form again (verses 7-8). The second word gives them the breath of life and makes them fully human (verses 9-10). The Hebrew word for *breath* may also be translated *spirit* (verses 1, 14) or *wind* (verse 9). This is literal breath and is also the life force which is the hallmark of a human being (see also Genesis 2:7).

The bones represent the people of Israel who see death on all sides and have given up hope for the future. Ezekiel's message to them is that God will raise them from their graves of exile and of despair. The issue of life and death is always in God's hands and God has declared that Israel will live.

Verses 15-28: Ezekiel is to perform another sign action (verses 16-17) and then interpret it for the exiles (verses 18-28). *Judah* represents the Southern Kingdom. *Joseph* and *Ephraim* represent the Northern Kingdom. *Israel* represents the combined people of Israel.

The people will be brought home to live under God's law with a king from the line of David. The Temple will be rebuilt and the covenant renewed. Israel will be sanctified, that is, set apart and made holy by God.

Oracles Against Gog (38:1–39:29)

Chapters 38 and 39 describe a future attack on Israel by heathen forces. God will intervene on Israel's side to destroy these attackers, and God's power will be made known to the nations of the earth. This decisive battle will come *after many days . . . in the latter* (NRSV) or *future* (NIV) *years* after the people of Israel are resettled in their homeland. The defeat of Gog is an ultimate reckoning with heathen nations in which no one will fail to understand that God's hand is at work in and through Israel.

The sequence of events in these oracles may be outlined as follows:

1. The armies of Gog will assemble and come against peaceful and prosperous Israel (38:1-16).
2. God will summon the powers of heaven and earth to destroy Gog's forces (38:17–39:8).
3. The people of Israel will burn the weapons of God and bury the bones of his warriors after the birds and beasts have feasted on the dead bodies (39:9-20).
4. Both Israel and the nations will then know the truth about Israel's exile and restoration (39:21-29).

Verses 1-16: Gog is a leader from the mountains of Asia Minor who commands a mighty army. (See the Glossary for place name identifications.)

In the future years (NIV) or *latter years* (NRSV) is a time after Ezekiel's prophecies of restoration for Israel have been fulfilled.

The *center of the earth* (NRSV) or *land* (NIV) is Jerusalem.

Ezekiel's prophetic word sets in motion the forces by which God will compel Gog to move against Israel.

Verses 17-23: The prophets *in former days* may include Jeremiah, who spoke of an enemy coming from the north (see Jeremiah 4:13; 6:22). These earlier prophecies are extended to apply to this future foe from the north. (The writer of Revelation 20:7-10 in turn reapplies Ezekiel's prophecy.)

Earthquake (see Isaiah 24:18-20), disease and bloodshed (see Ezekiel 5:16-17), and fire and brimstone (see Genesis 19:24) are acts of God's judgment.

Verses 39:1-8: The coming day of the Lord is one of destruction for the forces of evil. This day is also one of the revelation of God's power.

Verses 9-20: The people of Israel will warm themselves and cook their food for seven years over fires made from the weapons of Gog. They will work for seven months to bury the bones of the dead soldiers.

The bodies of the dead soldiers are to be a sacrificial offering for peace. The birds and beasts feast at God's victory table. The people of Israel, the birds, and the beasts are God's priests who cleanse and purify the land after Gog's defeat.

Verses 21-24: God's glory, that is, God's presence in all its holiness and power, will be at work among the nations and Israel. Everyone will know that Israel's past defeat came because God's benevolent presence was withdrawn (compare Numbers 6:24-26).

Verses 25-29: These verses summarize the promises of salvation and restoration for Israel that were given in chapters 34–37. They make a transition into the vision of the restored Temple and land which follows in chapters 40–48.

§ § § § § § §

The Message of Ezekiel 33–39

The prophet Jeremiah had told Israel of a foe from the north that would be the agent of God's judgment. In Jeremiah and Ezekiel's time this foe was Babylon. Ezekiel foresees a time when another foe from the north will come against the reunited people of Israel. This foe is from the mountains of Asia Minor in the area of Meshech-Tubal, a nation with whom Israel had dealings in the past (see Ezekiel 32:26). At an unnamed time in the future the power of God will bring this foe into battle with Israel. This is really God's battle, however, for the forces of nature and cosmic terror rather than Israelite warriors are decisive in Gog's defeat.

The people of Israel did return to their homeland under the direction of the Persian king Cyrus in 539 B.C. They lived under Persian rule until the Greeks defeated Persia and became the dominant world power. The cataclysmic battle with Gog has yet to take place in Israel.

The Revelation to John casts a battle with the forces of Gog in the future under different circumstances (see Revelation 20:7-10). Thus, precise identification of Gog or of the time of this great battle either in the past or the future is uncertain.

What conclusions can we draw from the prophecies of Ezekiel concerning the future for the people of God?

§ During the years of Ezekiel's prophecy the people of Israel had only God's word to turn to. Their political, economic, and military power were gone. Their land was devastated and under foreign control.

§ The prophetic word from Ezekiel and other prophets was that God was watching over God's word to perform it (see also Jeremiah 1:11-12).

§ God's word for Israel was one of both judgment and redemption.

§ Answers to their questions about the past and the future were in God's word to them.

§ The tension between judgment and promise, good and evil would be resolved in God's future.

§ The people of Israel had been set apart as the people of God. They, as representatives of God's kingdom on earth, would be triumphant.

§ § § § § § §

Ezekiel 40–44

Introduction to These Chapters

In Ezekiel 40–48 the prophet is shown the restored
Temple and the renewed land of Israel. The content of
this entire vision may be outlined as follows:
I. The Dimensions of the Temple (40:1–42:20)
II. God's Glory Returns to the Temple (43:1-12)
III. The Altar and Temple Regulations (43:13–44:31)
IV. Land Use and Community Regulations (45:1–46:24)
V. The Sacred River (47:1-12)
VI. The Boundaries of the New Israel (47:13–48:35)

Here is an outline of Ezekiel 40–44.
I. The Dimensions of the Temple (40:1–42:20)
   A. The Temple's gates and courts (40:1–41:4)
   B. A description of the Temple (41:5-26)
   C. The chambers and the walls (42:1-20)
II. God's Glory Returns to the Temple (43:1-12)
III. The Altar and Temple Regulations (43:13–44:31)

The Temple's Gates and Courts (40:1-49)

This new Temple is similar to Solomon's Temple,
which was burned in August 587 B.C. by the Babylonians.

Verses 1-4: Ezekiel is transported in visions to the
Temple mount in Jerusalem on April 28, 573 B.C. The
buildings that looked like a city (NIV) or *structure like a city*
(NRSV) is the Temple.

Verses 5-16: The heavenly guide carries a measuring

reed which is about ten feet and four inches long (based on a long or old standard cubit).

The gateway facing east is the main entrance to the Temple. Archeologists have found similar gateways in buildings from Solomon's reign. The side rooms within the gateway are probably to be used by priests who keep watch or control over those persons who enter the Temple.

Palm trees are commonly pictured in Near Eastern decorations.

Verses 17-27: The outer court is where the community assembles for worship.

The *thirty chambers* (NRSV) or *rooms* (NIV) may be used for sacrificial meals and as meeting rooms for Temple visitors.

Verses 28-37: Eight steps (approximately 8 feet in length) lead up from the outer court to the gates of the inner court. The Temple building itself is on top of a series of terraces.

Verses 38-46: These verses do not mention the heavenly guide or measurements and may be an editorial addition to the basic vision narrative.

The tables are used for washing and slaughtering sacrificial animals (see also Leviticus 1:1–7:38). The burnt (or whole) offering is completely burnt. The other offerings are divided so that some parts are burnt and other parts are eaten by the priests and the offerers. Sin offerings restore someone to purity. Guilt offerings atone for damage done to people or property.

Verses 40:47–41:4: The altar stands in the middle of the inner court in front of the Temple building.

The Temple is up approximately 10 feet from the inner court. The *pillars* may be freestanding columns.

The nave is the sanctuary or main room of the Temple. Only the guide goes into the inner room, which is the *most holy place.* This room is also known as the holy of holies. Since Ezekiel is a priest he may go into the nave but not the holy of holies. The high priest goes into this room once a year on the Day of Atonement (see Leviticus 16).

A Description of the Temple (41:5-26)

Verses 5-15: The side chambers of the Temple are three stories high and may be used for storage and for keeping Temple treasures.

Verses 15-26: These verses describe the interior decoration of the Temple. The paneling may be made of cedar.

Palm trees and cherubim (which are guardians of sacred places) were also used in decorations in Solomon's Temple.

Something resembling an altar (NRSV: which is only implied in NIV) is the table on which is put the bread of the Presence. Twelve loaves of bread are placed on the table each sabbath as a symbol of God's providing for the needs of the people.

The Chambers and Walls (42:1-20)

Verses 1-14: The priests' chambers are apparently built in three rows, terraced against the slope that rises from the outer court to the Temple level. The priests use these rooms to cook and eat their meals, to store their share of the sacrifices, and to change from the holy garments they wear for services into the common garments suitable for contact with people.

Verses 15-20: The outer walls are approximately 825 feet on each side. These walls are the boundary between the sacred, which is God's special place in the midst of God's people, and the common.

God's Glory Returns to the Temple (43:1-12)

The return of God's glory and the altar of burnt offering are described in these verses. Overwhelming sights and sounds accompany the vision of the glory of

God as God enters the Temple once more. The Temple is God's throne and God's dwelling place among the people. God's presence in the Temple is a sign and a confirmation of the renewed relationship between God and Israel.

The kings and the people will no longer worship idols. The Temple will only be used for the proper worship of God. The issue of *lifeless idols* (NIV) or *corpses* (NRSV) and *doorposts* (verses 7-8) may be related to the construction of the First Temple (Solomon's Temple). The north wall of the royal palace was the south wall of the Temple enclosure with a gate between the two areas. The Temple and palace could therefore be considered a single dwelling, and the death of a king in the palace would make the Temple unclean.

The Altar and Temple Regulations (43:13–44:31)

Verses 13-17: The altar of burnt offering looks like a series of steps resting on a foundation platform. The *altar hearth* is the top of the altar. The *horns* project upward from each corner of the top.

Verses 18-27: The new altar must be consecrated and cleansed (see also Exodus 29:36-37; Leviticus 8:14-15). Putting blood on the altar is part of an ancient covenant-making ceremony that symbolizes the uniting of God and God's people (see Exodus 24:6-7).

Atonement removes the effects of sin. After atonement, purification, and consecration the reconciliation between God and the people of Israel is complete. God then says, *I will accept you.*

The laws given in chapter 44 are about the people who will serve in the Temple. Some of this material may be from Ezekiel's disciples who were concerned with the Temple hierarchy.

Verses 1-3: The east gate remains shut as a sign of God's presence in the Temple. Only the prince may enter the east gateway from the court to eat a ceremonial meal.

Verses 4-14: Foreign slaves may no longer serve in the Temple (see Joshua 9:23; Numbers 31:30). They will be replaced by Levites, who are to be punished for worshiping idols by giving up some of their priestly duties (compare Deuteronomy 17:18–18:8).

Verses 15-27: The descendants of Zadok from the tribe of Levi are given the highest responsibilities in the Temple. They are to wear linen garments that are ritually pure. They are not to shave their heads or let their hair hang loose as people do in mourning. They may not drink intoxicating beverages before services, and they are not to marry a woman who might be considered unclean.

Priests' duties include teaching the people laws on purity. They act as judges because priests know civil and criminal law (see Deuteronomy 17:8-9) as well as religious and ceremonial law.

The livelihood of the priests will not depend on worldly possessions. God is to be their property or possession. Priests will receive food from the offerings and sacrifices that the people bring to the Temple. They will live on land which is part of the holy district set aside for the sanctuary (see Ezekiel 45:3-4; 48:10-12).

§ § § § § § §

The Message of Ezekiel 40–44

When the people of Israel are once again reunited in their homeland, the necessities of daily living must be provided for. These necessities include the rituals of worship and celebration. The instructions in Ezekiel 40–44 provide the basis on which Israel could become a worshiping community again.

§ Keeping in mind the abominations described in Ezekiel 8, these instructions provide protection for what is holy and sacred.
§ The holy and sacred is identified with and authenticated by the presence of God.
§ Shared ritual can bring the community of faith together and provide common ground on which they all may meet.

§ § § § § § §

Introduction to These Chapters

Chapters 45–48 include a description of land distribution, a long list of regulations concerning the prince, the observance of festivals, the habits of the priests, and a description of the boundaries of the new Israel.

Here is an outline of these chapters.

I. Creation of a Holy District (45:1-25)
II. Regulations for Prince and Priests (46:1-24)
III. The River and the Boundaries of Israel (47:1-23)
   A. The sacred river (47:1-12)
   B. The boundaries of the new Israel (47:13-23)
IV. Division of the Land and City (48:1-35)

Creation of a Holy District (45:1-25)

When the exiles return everyone must divide and use the land according to God's will.

Verses 1-8: Land is set aside for the Temple, for the priests, for the city of Jerusalem, and for the prince. The length is the east-west measurement. The width is the north-south measurement.

The land will no longer be divided according to the just or unjust wishes of the prince. God declares that land will be assigned to each of the tribes of Israel (see Ezekiel 48, where this is discussed in more detail).

Verses 9-17: The princes are warned against falling into the disobedience of former days. They are required to maintain just weights and measures in trade and in calculating Temple offerings. The prince receives the offerings from the people and then passes them on to the priests. The priests then offer the proper sacrifices for the people at appointed times.

Verses 18-25: Three festivals are mentioned here. The Day of Atonement is an annual ritual in which the Temple is cleansed from the contamination of human sin. The uncleanness is removed through sacrifices (verses 18-20).

Passover (verses 21-24), combined with the Feast of Unleavened Bread (see Exodus 23:15; Deuteronomy 16:1-8), is celebrated by a seven-day festival.

The prince will also provide offerings for the Harvest Festival celebrated in the fall (verse 25).

Regulations for Prince and Priests (46:1-24)

Verses 1-8: These verses give the regulations for celebrating the sabbath (verses 1-5) and the new moon (verses 6-8).

The rituals given for the sabbath show an increasing emphasis on this day. The sabbath is still to be a day of rest as in the past (see Exodus 20:8-11). It is also now to be a day of sacrifice and worship to affirm God's restoration and redemption of Israel.

The new moon celebration on the first day of each month is also to be a day of rest, of rejoicing, and of sacrifice.

Verses 9-10: For crowd control on feast days, worshipers are instructed to exit through the opposite door from which they entered the Temple court.

Verses 11-15: The prince may provide a freewill, or voluntary, offering in addition to the required daily burnt offerings.

Verses 16-18: Property of the prince cannot pass out of his family permanently nor can he take the property of others. The *year of liberty* (NRSV) or *freedom* (NIV) is the jubilee year (see Leviticus 25:8-17) in which leases expire and land goes back to its original family.

Verses 19-24: Ezekiel is shown more details of the

priests' quarters. *Consecrating people* (NIV) or to *communicate holiness* (NRSV) refers to the fact that the sacrifices are considered holy. They must not become unclean through contact with the outer court and the common worshipers.

In the outer court the Levites cook the sacrificial meals that are the worshipers' portion of the day's offerings. These worshipers must be ritually clean to enter the Temple, but are not sanctified to enter the inner court.

The Sacred River (47:1-12)

Ezekiel is shown a sacred river that springs from beneath the Temple and flows eastward into the desert and then to the Dead Sea.

Verses 1-2: The water comes from under the throne of God, the most holy site of God's presence in Israel.

Verses 3-12: The small stream becomes a mighty river as it flows toward the Dead Sea. As it flows it brings bountiful life to the desert wastelands and to the salty waters of the sea. The Dead Sea will become fresh so that fish may live in it as they do in the Mediterranean (the *Great Sea*). The swamps and marshes will remain salty, however, so that salt may still be extracted from the water.

The land and the people enjoy strength, fruitfulness, and healing.

The Boundaries of the New Israel (47:13-23)

Only territory west of the Jordan River is included, perhaps because this is the land promised to the patriarchs (see Numbers 34:1-12). An *inheritance* means the possession of land which is handed down by right of descent. The land belongs to God and is held in trust by the people of Israel as a gift.

Each of the tribes will receive an equal portion of land without regard for its size or for geographical considerations. A tribe is generally a unit of families or clans related by blood.

Verses 15-20: Some of the places named here cannot be located with certainty. See the map for the location of those that can be identified.

Verses 21-23: Resident aliens in Israel had previously not been allowed to own land but had legal protection under the law. These instructions in Ezekiel allow resident aliens more participation and a more permanent status in the community of faith.

Division of the Land and City (48:1-35)

Verses 1-7, 23-29: The tribes are named for the sons of Jacob (see Genesis 35:22-26). The tribes of Manasseh and Ephraim, the sons of Joseph, are named instead of Levi, the priestly tribe, which is to have land within the holy district (verse 12). Each tribe has an equal portion of land that stretches from the western to the eastern borders and is approximately 8.3 miles from north to south. The tribes named for the sons of Jacob's wives, rather than sons of his concubines, receive portions closest to the holy district.

Verses 8-22: The central portion of land belongs to the prince, to the city of Jerusalem, and to the holy district including the Temple and priestly land.

Jerusalem is to be a square, 1.6 miles on each side, which is ten times the size of the Temple. The city and the open country around it are for ordinary use apart from the sacred area which is holy to the Lord.

Verses 30-35: Each of the gates in the city walls is named for a tribe, thus representing all of the nation of Israel. Here Manasseh and Ephraim are replaced by Joseph (their father) and Levi.

The name *Jerusalem* means *founded peaceful.* This city will now be called *The* LORD *is there.* Though the city is outside the holy district in the previous verses, Jerusalem is blessed by God's presence and honored to be God's dwelling place (see also Psalm 46; Isaiah 60:14).

§ § § § § § §

The Message of Ezekiel 45–48

The new name of Jerusalem is a symbol of the renewed relationship between God and the people of God. Now they may once again dwell together. Ezekiel 40–48 gives a structure by which the people are to live out their relationship with God. The purpose behind this structure can be seen in the regulations about religious festivals. Through these rituals and ceremonies the people of Israel are to:

- maintain the purity of God's sanctuary,
- remember how God called them out of slavery to be God's people,
- celebrate the bounty of the land which God gave them.

This new life is not the creation of the people. Rather, it comes from God and is God's gracious gift. This life-giving gift is symbolized in the river that flows from the Temple (God's dwelling) out into the land.

§ Both the people and the land are transformed by God's gift.

§ This new reality is not other-worldly. It is based on Israel's historical experience with God.

§ The new life is to be lived in this world in real time.

§ This transformation goes beyond normal expectations of fruitfulness and security, however, because Israel's new life is like a return to paradise (see Genesis 1–2). These expectations have not yet been fulfilled in human history (see Revelation 22:1-5).

§ § § § § § §

Conclusions on the Book of Ezekiel

Ezekiel's idealized Israel was not created when the exiles were allowed to return home in 539 B.C. Many of them stayed in Babylonia where, in later years, the Babylonian-Israelite community became an influential force in world Judaism.

The instructions for the new Israel do, however, offer a perspective from which the community of faith is to be set up in the Promised Land:

§ God is to be Israel's sanctuary.

§ All life must center on and flow from God.

§ The land and its bounty are to be shared equally, even with foreigners.

From an even broader perspective, Ezekiel shows the people of God how they may move successfully into the future:

§ They must recognize and honestly accept the failures of the past.

§ They must pass through the stages of recognition, acceptance, grief, and repentance in order to move into new life.

§ They must recommit themselves to live under the covenant.

§ They must be open to God's new creation in them and through them.

As a prophet, Ezekiel calls into question people's assumptions about God and about what it means to live a life of faith. He proclaims that God's future for the community of faith comes through recollection, reconciliation, and expectation. Above all, Ezekiel demands that God's people, both then and now, accept God's reality and God's future for their lives.

§ § § § § § §

Introduction to Daniel

Like Ezekiel, Daniel was an exile caught up in the struggle between mighty Babylon and tiny Judah.

The book of Daniel tells of events in Daniel's life as an exile and tells of visions that came to Daniel from God. The overall perspective of these visions and stories is that underlying all earthly reality is God's reality. That is, both history and time are subject to God's control; and no one—king, captive, or peasant, those who are wise or are unknowing, angelic prince or human being—may escape the influence of God's dominion.

Daniel the Book

The book of Daniel is a collection of stories and vision reports. Chapters 1–6 are stories about Daniel and his friends in Babylon. Chapters 7–12 tell of Daniel's visions.

Part of the book is written in Hebrew, the language of Israel (Daniel 1:1–2:4a and 8:1–12:13). The rest of the book is written in Aramaic (Daniel 2:4b–7:28), which was the international language of Daniel's day.

The stories and visions in the Aramaic chapters demonstrate that God is Lord of all peoples and that God's power is greater than the power of any earthly ruler. The Hebrew chapters place Daniel and his friends in Babylon and tell how world events will affect Jerusalem and God's chosen people.

Through dramatic and sometimes obscure symbolism the vision reports in Daniel reveal some of God's plan for "the end" of the age. Because of this, these visions have been called *apocalyptic* (from a Greek word meaning *revelation*) and *eschatological* (from a Greek word meaning *end*).

The book contains stories told by Daniel and stories told about him. Daniel 7:1 says that Daniel himself wrote an account of one of his visions. Daniel may have written others or he may have dictated these accounts to a scribe. The Israelites took their sacred writings with them into exile and they continued in Babylon to practice their scribal traditions of recording history (for example, Jeremiah 52), prophecy (for example, Ezekiel 20), and hymns (for example, Psalm 137).

These stories and vision reports could have been recorded in part during Daniel's lifetime and then collected and arranged in their present form after his death.

Historical Circumstances

Who wrote the book of Daniel and when it was written are matters of dispute, however. Many of the earliest Jewish and Christian interpreters of Daniel believed Daniel to be a prophet and accepted the book as Scripture that came from the Exile.

Later interpreters believed that the book of Daniel was written during the Maccabean period which was the second century B.C. (approximately 170-165) in Palestine. They believed that Daniel best reflects the conflict of that time between the Jews and the Greek tyrant Antiochus IV. In this case, Daniel would have been written by someone using Daniel's name and holding Daniel up as an example of a pious and wise man from the past. This would make the book of Daniel prophecy "after the fact." The purpose of such prophecy would have been to instruct and encourage the Jews in their struggle against Greek oppression.

Recent discoveries in the fields of ancient Near Eastern history, archeology, and language suggest that the book of Daniel did originate in the Babylonian Exile. (This evidence is included in the commentary sections.) Current scholarship, however, is still divided between the views that Daniel came out of Babylon in the fifth or sixth century B.C. and that the book came from Judah in the third or second century B.C.

Whenever Daniel was written, it is obvious that the book came out of a community under stress. In the face of warfare and oppression, the community of God's people naturally would ask "What does all this mean?" In answering this question, Daniel offers God's people a particular way to look at the world. Daniel's perspective is that all reality, both earthly and heavenly, is under God's dominion. Therefore, God's people may face the world and the future with confidence.

The additions to the book of Daniel are stories, a prayer, and a hymn. They are found in Daniel in the Septuagint, a Greek translation of the Old Testament which was begun in the third century B.C. in Egypt. These additions are accepted as Scripture by the Roman Catholic Church but are assigned to the Apocrypha by the Protestant Church.

Daniel the Man

What we know of Daniel's personal background comes from Daniel 1:3-4.

Daniel was from an honored and privileged Israelite family. This may be one of the reasons that he was taken to Babylon in 605 B.C. In 598 B.C. and 587 B.C. the Babylonians also took many Israelite leaders and artisans into exile. When he went to live in Babylon, Daniel was probably in his late teens. He was a well-educated, intelligent, and handsome young man.

Like most upper-class Israelite boys of his time, Daniel's education probably began at home where he was taught the history of his people and of God's covenant with Israel. He was probably also instructed in the ethical conduct of life as well as in reading and writing.

During his time in Babylon, Daniel learned the Babylonian language and script and was probably taught Babylonian history as well. He became an able administrator in the governments of Babylon and Persia and led a prosperous life.

The Israelites brought their sacred writings with them into exile, and Daniel continued to study them. He also observed the personal rituals of his faith, such as prayer, meditation, and fasting.

Daniel knew about dreams and about their interpretation. He had visions from God concerning great mysteries. He was a man of courage and conviction. Though he knew how to flourish in a pagan society, he also continued to live out his faith in God.

Indeed, the fundamental fact about Daniel is his reliance on God. Daniel was an outstanding man who is renowned to later generations for his wisdom and courage. Yet, it is to God that Daniel gave the praise and credit for all his accomplishments.

VISIONS IN DANIEL

CHAPTER 2	CHAPTER 7	CHAPTER 8	CHAPTERS 10–12
The Great Image	**The Four Beasts**	**Ram and He-Goat**	**A Word for Latter Days**
Gold (Babylon, Daniel 2:38)	**Lion** (Daniel 7:4)	**Ram** (Media-Persia, Daniel 8:20)	**Persia** (Daniel 11:2)
Silver (Media-Persia? Daniel 2:39)	**Bear** (Daniel 7:5)	**Goat** (Greece, Daniel 8:21)	
Bronze (Greece? Daniel 2:39)	**Leopard** (Daniel 7:6)		**Greece** (Daniel 11:3-4; also 11:5-45?)
Iron/Clay (Rome? Daniel 2:40)	**Indescribable Beast** (Daniel 7:7-8)		**Rome** (or *the western coastlands* in the NIV and *Kittim* in the NRSV) (coming to power, Daniel 11:29-30)
Supernatural Stone/God's Kingdom	**Kingdom of the Son of Man and of the Saints**		"The end of the days" (Daniel 12:1-13)

Daniel 1–3

Introduction to These Chapters

Daniel 1–3 is a collection of stories about Daniel and his Jewish friends in Nebuchadnezzar's court. Chapter 1 introduces the Hebrew youths and explains when and how they came to Babylon. Chapter 2 tells of Daniel's role in interpreting a dream for King Nebuchadnezzar. Chapter 3 is the story of Shadrach, Meshach, and Abednego in the fiery furnace.

Here is an outline of these chapters.

I. Daniel and His Friends (1:1-21)
   A. Introduction (1:1-2)
   B. The youths get special treatment (1:3-7)
   C. The Hebrew youths are tested (1:8-16)
   D. The Hebrew youths excel in wisdom (1:17-21)
II. Nebuchadnezzar's Vision (2:1-49)
   A. Nebuchadnezzar has a dream (2:1-11)
   B. The Hebrew youths seek God's help (2:12-23)
   C. Daniel tells Nebuchadnezzar's dream (2:24-35)
   D. The interpretation of the dream (2:36-45)
   E. Outcome for Daniel and his friends (2:46-49)
III. The Fiery Furnace (3:1-30)
   A. Nebuchadnezzar's image of gold (3:1-2)
   B. The summons to worship the image (3:3-7)
   C. Accusations against the Jews (3:8-12)
   D. The youths refuse the king's order (3:13-18)
   E. Four men walk in the fire (3:19-25)
   F. The faithful youths are rewarded (3:26-30)

Introduction (1:1-2)

These verses introduce the book as a whole as well as the first chapter. The setting and time for the beginning of Daniel's story are established.

The *third year* of Jehoiakim is 605 B.C. Jeremiah 25:1 says that Jehoiakim's fourth year as king of Judah is Nebuchadnezzar's first year as king of Babylon. Jeremiah and Daniel are apparently both correct because they use different systems of dating these events.

The Babylonian method of record-keeping does not count the months between a king's coronation and the next new year as part of his official reign. The months between September 605 B.C. and April 604 B.C. are known as Nebuchadnezzar's ascension year. Daniel uses this Babylonian method of dating.

Jeremiah uses the method common in Judah, which counts the ascension months as the first year. Thus, Jehoiakim's third year as king (Daniel) and fourth year as king (Jeremiah) are 605 B.C.

The Youths Get Special Treatment (1:3-7)

The chief eunuch is in charge of the king's harems and of the education of royal young people.

The Hebrew youths (children or adolescents) were probably brought to Babylon and to the palace because of their beauty and intelligence. In the deportations of 597 B.C. and 587 B.C. the Babylonians took the leading citizens and artisans of Jerusalem into exile. Daniel and his friends may have been taken to Babylon in 605 B.C. both as a gesture of Nebuchadnezzar's power over Judah and as potential servants in Nebuchadnezzar's government.

The further education of the Hebrew youths is to make them able servants (able to enter the king's court or service) of their new master. This education may include the study of literature, language, astrology, astronomy, math, and medicine.

Daniel and his friends are given Babylonian names. This is probably a convenience for the Babylonians and a symbol of their transition into a new rank and a new life.

The Hebrew Youths Are Tested (1:8-16)

Daniel accepts his new position in the king's household, accepts a new name and a Babylonian education, but he will not accept the king's rich food. This rich food is a gift of honor from the king's table, but Daniel refuses the gift.

Eating some of this food (pork, for example) would violate the dietary laws of Daniel's faith (see Deuteronomy 14; Leviticus 11). Also, refusing this food is a way of putting some distance between himself and Nebuchadnezzar. In ancient times, shared meals were a sign of friendship, and covenant ceremonies sometimes included meals. By refusing the gift of rich food, Daniel refuses to give unconditional loyalty to Nebuchadnezzar.

The combination of God's favor (verse 9) and a vegetarian diet (verse 12) makes the Hebrew youths healthier than the rest of their fellow students. So the steward keeps on taking away the rich food.

The Hebrew Youths Excel in Wisdom (1:17-21)

The story again affirms that God is at work in the lives of Daniel and his friends. They are ten times more wise than the Babylonian practitioners of magical arts because wisdom given by God is always ten times better than human wisdom alone. The number ten symbolizes completeness.

The youths, particularly Daniel, are more wise in every way. Daniel has special insight into dreams and visions, into a different dimension of reality. Thus, the stage is set for what happens in the rest of the book.

Verse 21 says that Daniel was there (perhaps meaning in the city of Babylon) until the first year of Cyrus, the king of Persia (539/538 B.C.).

Nebuchadnezzar's Vision (2:1-49)

This story tells how Daniel, with help from his friends and with wisdom from God, interprets a dream for Nebuchadnezzar.

Nebuchadnezzar Has a Dream (2:1-11)

The second year of Nebuchadnezzar's reign (603/602 B.C.) is Daniel's third year in Babylon.

In verse 4 the Hebrew text says, *the astrologers* (NIV) or *Chaldeans* (NRSV) spoke *to the king in Aramaic* . . . The text then continues in Aramaic, *O King* . . ., through Daniel 7:28. This is the longest section of Aramaic in the Old Testament.

Aramaic was the international language of the ancient Near East by the eighth century B.C. The Aramaic used in the book of Daniel has been identified as "official Aramaic" which was in use in the region from approximately 700–300 B.C.

The Babylonian wise men want Nebuchadnezzar to tell them his dream so that they may talk together and consult their dream books about an interpretation. Such dream books record many past dreams and the events which followed them as a guide for interpreting future dreams.

Nebuchadnezzar does not trust these men because they would lie to buy time and to save themselves until circumstances change. Perhaps they hope the king will forget about his disturbing dream.

The Hebrew Youths Seek God's Help (2:12-23)

Daniel and his companions are included in the company of wise men (as they are in 1:8-20) to be slain. But they are not in the group asked for an interpretation of the king's dream. Daniel acts quickly to resolve the crisis.

The four faithful Hebrew youths must seek God's mercy and wisdom to solve this problem.

Their prayer brings Daniel a revelation, and, in response, Daniel offers a hymn of praise and thanks to God (verses 20-23). He speaks of God's eternal nature (verses 20-21) and of God's help in this particular situation (verse 23).

Daniel Tells Nebuchadnezzar's Dream (2:24-35)

Daniel's first statement to Nebuchadnezzar places the dream and its interpretation in their proper contexts—God is at work in this situation. Both Nebuchadnezzar and Daniel owe what wisdom they may gain from all this to God's wisdom and God's gracious revelation.

Nebuchadnezzar had gone to bed thinking about the future, and his dream concerned *the days to come* (NIV) or *the end of days* (NRSV). Elsewhere in the Old Testament, the latter days sometimes refer to the end of the age and sometimes refer in a more general way to certain decisive days in the future.

The latter days in Nebuchadnezzar's dream reveal the end of the present world order and the coming of God's kingdom (verses 44-45).

In his dream, Nebuchadnezzar saw a great human-like statue made of different metals.

The Interpretation of the Dream (2:36-45)

Daniel tells Nebuchadnezzar what the dream means. He proclaims Nebuchadnezzar's power and might as king but makes it clear that this power is a gift from God. The metals of the statue represent human kingdoms. Only the head of gold is specifically identified. The other metals of diminishing value represent kingdoms which will come after Nebuchadnezzar.

Scholars have differing opinions about which kingdoms these other metals represent. The kingdom of silver may be the Median kingdom (Daniel 5:31; 6:1; 9:1) or the combined kingdom of Media and Persia (Daniel

5:28; 6:8; 8:20). The bronze kingdom may be Persia (Daniel 1:21; 6:28; 10:1) or Greece (Daniel 8:21). The iron and clay kingdom may be Greece or Rome (called *Kittim* [NRSV] or *the western coastlands* [NIV] in Daniel 11:30). Verse 43 refers to marriages among the ruling families of the fourth kingdom.

In this vision, the stone that destroys the statue and grows into a mountain is a reference to the kingdom of God. God's kingdom will replace all human kingdoms, and in the future God's people will no longer live under foreign rule (nor will it *be left to another people*). This shall be an eternal kingdom in contrast to the human kingdoms which all will eventually come to an end.

The statue as a whole is a symbol for all human power. Though it is divided into kingdoms which follow one another, the whole statue falls at once. This shows that all human power is and will be overwhelmed and replaced by God's power.

The birth of Jesus may be the stone and mountain which mark the coming of God's kingdom. In that case, the kingdom of iron and clay is the Roman Empire. This would mean that the dream has been fulfilled to some extent in history, though not all human kingdoms have been destroyed. The complete fulfillment of God's eternal kingdom is in the future (see, for example, Daniel 7:27).

This stone or mountain is similar to God's holy mountain elsewhere in the Old Testament (see Genesis 28:10-22; 49:24; Psalm 118:22; Isaiah 28:16) and to the cornerstone of the New Testament (Matthew 21:42; Mark 12:10; Luke 20:17; Acts 4:11).

Outcome for Daniel and His Friends (2:46-49)

Nebuchadnezzar's gifts and homage to Daniel also honor Daniel's God who revealed the mystery. Daniel is appointed as governor over the province which includes the capital city, and he is also made the "chairman of the board" of the wise men.

The Fiery Furnace (3:1-30)

In this narrative Shadrach, Meshach, and Abednego face the ordeal of the fiery furnace.

Nebuchadnezzar's Image of Gold (3:1-2)

The image of gold is approximately ninety feet tall and nine feet wide and is dedicated to one of Babylon's gods. Such huge images were common in the ancient Near East.

The officials who are called to the dedication of the image are administrative and judicial personnel in the government. The name *Satrap* is an Old Persian title for the head official of a region. Since Old Persian was in use until approximately 300 B.C., the use of this word in Daniel suggests that this story was written before 300 B.C.

Vassal kings may have also been summoned to this dedication. King Zedekiah of Judah visited Babylon in 593 B.C. (see Jeremiah 51:59-64), perhaps to pledge his continued loyalty to Nebuchadnezzar.

The Summons to Worship the Image (3:3-7)

Worshiping the image is to be a sign of loyalty to the king. Failure to worship is taken as an act of treason.

The blazing *furnace* is a kiln with openings at the top and bottom.

Accusations Against the Jews (3:8-12)

The Chaldean informers wish to be rid of Shadrach, Meshach, and Abednego. Daniel is not included in the summons to worship the image, perhaps because he is out of the district at the time and does not hear the command.

The Youths Refuse the King's Order (3:13-18)

Shadrach, Meshach, and Abednego brush aside Nebuchadnezzar's threatening questions, but they answer him anyway. They confess their faith in God and proclaim that God's power is greater than the king's power over them. They also admit that God may not save them, perhaps because they do not feel worthy to be saved.

Four Men Walk in the Fire (3:19-25)

After the men are thrown into the furnace, Nebuchadnezzar sees them loosed from their bonds and walking around. The fourth man is a heavenly being or angel who has been sent to comfort and protect them.

The Faithful Youths Are Rewarded (3:26-30)

Nebuchadnezzar calls the men out of the furnace and offers praise to their God. In blessing God, the king admits there is a power greater than his own. He also testifies to Shadrach, Meshach, and Abednego's faithfulness.

The king's decree protects God's name from blasphemy and God's servants from harm. The king does not, however, give up his other gods.

Shadrach, Meshach, and Abednego's lives are spared and they receive material reward for their faithfulness. The story of their rescue testifies that God is free to work in the world and that God sometimes does this in surprising ways. All the stories, visions, and prayers in Daniel announce God's power and freedom.

§ § § § § § §

The Message of Daniel 1–3

Daniel 1 introduces the time, setting, and circumstances for the book of Daniel. This chapter establishes the high character and faithfulness of Daniel and his friends. Chapters 2–3 also testify to their devotion to God and to the rewards that follow. These are very personal stories of faith and of conflict.

These are more than exciting stories, however. These stories have a larger perspective than just the individuals involved. God's action and will are in each one. What do these stories tell us about God?

§ God is Lord of all peoples and is greater than all human power.

§ God's rule is eternal.

§ God directs the course of human history.

§ God is present in a foreign land as well as in Jerusalem.

§ God is in relationship to all peoples.

§ God reveals mysteries to believers and to nonbelievers. The believer is a source of knowledge to the nonbeliever.

§ God's faithful servants are rewarded.

§ God's wisdom is available to those who earnestly seek it.

§ These qualities of God's nature and action are proclaimed throughout the book of Daniel.

§ § § § § § §

Daniel 4–6

Introduction to These Chapters

Daniel 4–6 tells of Daniel's dealings with three different kings—Nebuchadnezzar, Belshazzar, and Darius. In each case, Daniel's God-given wisdom and devotion are tested and proved.

Here is an outline of these chapters.

I. Signs and Wonders Shown (4:1-37)
   A. Nebuchadnezzar praises God (4:1-3)
   B. The dream (4:4-18)
   C. The interpretation (4:19-27)
   D. The fulfillment (4:28-33)
   E. Nebuchadnezzar's restoration (4:34-37)

II. The Handwriting on the Wall (5:1-31)
   A. Belshazzar's feast (5:1-2)
   B. A hand writes on the wall (5:3-9)
   C. Daniel interprets the writing (5:10-16)
   D. Daniel condemns the king (5:17-23)
   E. The message (5:24-28)
   F. The end for Babylonia (5:29-31)

III. Daniel in the Lions' Den (6:1-28)
   A. Daniel's place under Darius (6:1-3)
   B. The plot (6:4-9)
   C. Daniel is trapped (6:10-13)
   D. Daniel's night in the lions' den (6:14-18)
   E. Daniel's rescue (6:19-24)
   F. Daniel prospers (6:25-28)

Signs and Wonders Shown (4:1-37)

Nebuchadnezzar issues a proclamation to the people of his kingdom telling them of a dream he had, of its interpretation, and of its fulfillment.

Nebuchadnezzar Praises God (4:1-3)

After everything Nebuchadnezzar has been through, he offers this short hymn of praise to God.

Signs and wonders are actions that testify to God's power and confirm God's word (see also Deuteronomy 4:34).

The Dream (4:4-18)

Nebuchadnezzar is at the height of his power. He is at ease and prospering in his reign as ruler of a huge empire. A disturbing dream makes him afraid, however. He dreams of a great world-tree (see also Ezekiel 17:22-24; 31:1-11) at the center of the earth on which all life depends (verses 10-12).

The *messenger* (NIV) or *watcher* (NRSV) is a heavenly being who is a representative of the Most High and who carries out the sentence of the heavenly council (verse 17).

The band of iron and bronze around the tree stump may symbolize Nebuchadnezzar's coming bondage or may be a symbol that Nebuchadnezzar's kingdom will be kept waiting for him (see verse 27).

In verse 15 *it* (the tree) changes to *him* (a man). The symbol of the great tree is replaced by a man who loses his mind and becomes beast-like. Similar cases of this type of mental illness are known from both prescientific and modern times.

Seven times (verse 16) may mean seven years or seven seasons.

The watcher announces the message of the dream in verse 18—the tree/man is to be an example for all people. Everyone must know that God controls human rulers.

God gives power even to those who sink so low as to act like a beast of the field.

Nebuchadnezzar turns to Daniel for an interpretation because Daniel has spiritual knowledge which is greater than human knowledge.

The Interpretation (4:19-27)

Daniel's wish that the dream not affect Nebuchadnezzar may be a common statement of the times expressing a wish to avoid bad tidings. This statement also shows that Nebuchadnezzar will have a chance to avoid the consequences of the dream.

Daniel's interpretation confirms that Nebuchadnezzar is a great and powerful king. The king's power is not the issue. The problem is that Nebuchadnezzar must acknowledge a power greater than himself at whose pleasure he rules (verse 25).

Daniel urges Nebuchadnezzar to change his ways and do what is right. Nebuchadnezzar's sin is unfounded pride in his own accomplishments. He has failed to admit his proper place under God's dominion.

Practicing righteousness and showing mercy are good works which would be evidence that Nebuchadnezzar has broken from sin. If he refuses to heed this warning, he will lose the freedom he enjoys as a human being and will be bound in a beast-like life.

The Fulfillment (4:28-33)

Here we see that Nebuchadnezzar's boast of self-satisfaction is not even out of his mouth before his dream becomes a reality.

The phrase *this great* (NIV) or *magnificent* (NRSV) *Babylon* has been found in inscriptions from Nebuchadnezzar's reign. Archeologists have also found buildings from his time all over Babylon. The king's claim to have built such a great city is justified, but his arrogance and his lack of respect for God's power bring his punishment.

No document now available other than the book of Daniel speaks of Nebuchadnezzar's madness. However, part of a Babylonian tablet now in the British museum hints that Nebuchadnezzar may have left his throne and family for a time and that his son may have ruled in his place.

Nebuchadnezzar's Restoration (4:34-37)

The *end of that time* (NIV) or *when that period was over* (NRSV) is the end of the *seven times.*

Nebuchadnezzar, even in his madness, keeps enough of his humanity so that he can lift his eyes to heaven. This gesture of humility is a response and appeal to God, who allows Nebuchadnezzar to become fully human again. With his mind healed, the king offers a hymn of praise and honor to God (for similar hymns, see also Psalm 145:3; Isaiah 45:8; Jeremiah 10:10). He confesses God's power over heaven and earth (but probably still holds to his other gods).

The Handwriting on the Wall (5:1-31)

Daniel 5 is the famous "handwriting on the wall" story. King Belshazzar receives a message from God on the night that Babylon falls to the Medes and Persians.

Belshazzar's Feast (5:1-2)

Belshazzar is the ruler in Babylon in 539 B.C. when the city falls to the forces of Darius the Mede.

King Nabonidus is Belshazzar's actual father. King Nebuchadnezzar, who is called Belshazzar's father (verse 2), may have been his grandfather. In Semitic languages such as Aramaic, "father" may refer to one's actual father, to one's grandfather, to another remote ancestor, or to a predecessor in office.

Belshazzar is apparently acting as king during

Nabonidus's absence. Babylonian historical documents state that Nabonidus entrusted Belshazzar with kingship and was away from Babylon for ten years (approximately 550/549 B.C. to 539 B.C.). Nabonidus was not in Babylon when the city was captured in October of 539 B.C.

Ancient Greek writers tell of a great feast in Babylon on the night of its fall. One writer says that this feast as well as the poor communication system within the large city contributed to the Babylonian defeat.

A Hand Writes on the Wall (5:3-9)

Belshazzar and the members of his court show their contempt for Israel's God by drinking from the holy vessels and praising their idols. This blasphemy immediately provokes a reaction from God. A man's hand appears and writes a message on the plaster walls. Archeologists have found such white plastered rooms in Babylonian excavations.

The phrase *will be made the third highest ruler* (NIV) may also be translated *shall rule as one of three* or *and rank third* (NRSV). Nabonidus and Belshazzar would be first and second in the kingdom with the interpreter promised a place of power next to them.

Purple clothing is expensive because of the difficulty in producing the purple dye. Purple is worn by those of wealth and high rank.

Daniel Interprets the Writing (5:10-16)

The *queen* is possibly Belshazzar's grandmother, Nebuchadnezzar's widow.

Daniel may have had a lower position in the Babylonian court after Nebuchadnezzar's death and may not have been known to King Belshazzar. Nevertheless, Belshazzar offers Daniel the same reward for the interpretation of the writing as he offers the other wise men.

Daniel Condemns the King (5:17-23)

Daniel reads the writing (verse 25), he interprets it (verses 26-28), and he tells the king why the writing appeared (verses 18-24). The reasons for the writing are as important as its interpretation. These reasons are part of the lesson to be learned by the king and by all those listening to Daniel.

Daniel refuses Belshazzar's promise of reward (verse 17), though in the end he is given the rewards anyway (verse 29). Daniel knows that even such extravagant gifts are meaningless in comparison to the power of God.

Daniel reminds Belshazzar of what happened to Nebuchadnezzar (verses 18-19, 21) and why it happened (verse 20). Belshazzar knows this but is arrogant enough to ignore the truth about God that was learned by Nebuchadnezzar.

Belshazzar has not humbled his heart toward God. Nor, apparently, has he humbled himself toward his fellow human beings. In the Old Testament, a person's heart is considered to be the source of a person's character. The heart is the place from which spring his or her hopes, fears, attitudes, and beliefs, as well as physical and intellectual powers.

In the Old Testament, to be humble is not to think less of oneself as a person. Rather, to be humble means to see oneself in right relationship to God and to other people.

The people of Israel remember their time as slaves. They also remember that God saved them and made them a community out of divine love and power, not because of their own merit or power. Thus, to be humble before God means to live by the belief that all wealth and power belong to and come from God. To be humble also involves one's relationships with others. It means not oppressing those who have less wealth or power than you do (see also Jeremiah 9:22-24).

Belshazzar is proud and does not see his proper place in life. He is also openly hostile to God. Daniel also says that Belshazzar is ignorant. He worships inanimate objects instead of the living God who controls the very breath of life.

The Message (5:24-28)

The message may have been written as a puzzle in Aramaic with the words arranged in three lines with five letters to a line. To read the message, the words are read from top to bottom rather than from right to left as they usually are.

Each word, depending on the vowels added to the consonants, can be either a noun or a verb. Daniel's interpretation of the message is based on the verbal forms of the words.

Mene means to count or number. *Tekel* means to weigh. *Parsin* (the plural of *peres*) means to divide.

The double *mene* may refer to the fact that Nabonidus and Belshazzar shared the throne. The days of both are numbered.

Belshazzar has been examined and a judgment made against him based on the evidence given in verses 22-23. God is giving the Babylonian kingdom to the Medes and Persians just as the rebellious kingdom of Israel had been given to the Babylonians.

The End for Babylonia (5:29-31)

By rewarding Daniel, God's spokesman, Belshazzar may hope to avoid the coming punishment.

The army of the Medes and Persians overran Babylon on the night of October 11/12 539 B.C. The Greek historian Xenophon recorded that a king (whom he does not name) was killed in the Babylonian palace the night the city was captured.

There has been a great deal of scholarly debate over the identity of Darius the Mede (verse 31). No record of a person by this name has been found outside of Daniel. He is not Darius I, king of Persia (522–486 B.C.). The name

Darius is used as a proper name or as a title by several Persian kings.

Darius the Mede may be the general who took Babylon for Cyrus and who administered the territory of Babylon. Such a general is known in history but by another name.

Daniel 9:1 says that Darius *became* or *was made* king over Babylon, so he may have been a vassal king under King Cyrus of Persia for most of the first year after the fall of Babylon. Ancient Persian documents record that Cyrus did not assume the title King of Babylon until some months after the city fell.

Daniel 5 ends with the fulfillment of the prophecies concerning Babylon spoken by Jeremiah (Jeremiah 51:11, 28) and Isaiah (Isaiah 13:17-19).

Daniel in the Lions' Den (6:1-28)

Daniel in the lions' den is similar to the fiery furnace story in Daniel 3. Both narratives testify that steadfastness in the faith is required of God's servants and that this steadfastness leads to life.

Daniel's Place Under Darius (6:1-3)

Each satrap administers a province in the kingdom. The presidents supervise them to be sure the king's interests are well served. Daniel outshines all the other officials because the spirit of God is with him to give him wisdom (see also Daniel 1:17; 2:47; 5:12).

The Plot (6:4-9)

Professional jealousy leads the other officials to hatch a clever plot against Daniel. Darius agrees to their petition, perhaps to strengthen his new position as king.

Other Scripture (Esther 8:8) and ancient historians also tell how the law of the Medes and Persians cannot be revoked once it is established.

Daniel Is Trapped (6:10-13)

Daniel maintains the disciplines of his faith which have sustained him in the past.

The practice of praying toward Jerusalem may have begun in Solomon's prayer in 1 Kings 8:30. The tradition of daily prayer in the morning, afternoon, and evening is said to have begun with Moses.

Daniel's Night in the Lions' Den (6:14-18)

Darius is grieved over the consequences of his ruling but is powerless to change it. In the end, he and Daniel both must trust God to intervene on Daniel's behalf.

Both the Assyrians and the Persians kept lions in zoological gardens. The lions' den into which Daniel was thrown probably was a pit or cave.

Daniel's Rescue (6:19-24)

Darius's anxious question to Daniel is also a confession. He confesses that Daniel serves a living God, but he is not sure that God is powerful enough to be able to save Daniel.

Daniel is innocent of any wrongdoing either toward God or toward Darius. Because he is innocent and because he trusts God (verse 23), God's angel saves him. God's power overrules the so-called irrevocable law of the Medes and Persians.

This story, as well as the fiery furnace story, proclaims God's freedom to act in ways humans might never guess. The present situation or reality is not absolute because God's future is not necessarily a continuation of the present. God breaks into time and space to make changes according to God's will.

Daniel Prospers (6:25-28)

Darius issues another decree which makes respect and esteem for the power of God lawful in his kingdom. His hymn of praise to God is similar to the hymns in Daniel 2:20-23 and 4:34-35. This hymn reflects what Darius has learned about God from Daniel—that is, God, not Darius, lives and rules forever.

Daniel's faithfulness, honesty, and administrative ability continue to serve him well in the future.

King Cyrus II of Persia inherited his kingdom from his father and began to expand his kingdom by conquest in 550 B.C. After capturing Babylonia, Cyrus issued a decree allowing the exiled Jews to return to their homeland and to rebuild the Temple (see Ezra 6:3-5). The prophet Isaiah saw Cyrus as the Lord's anointed in God's plan for history (see Isaiah 44:28; 45:1).

§ § § § § § §

The Message of Daniel 4–6

The stories in Daniel 4–6 show Daniel in very dramatic circumstances. Within these circumstances he shows us a life well-lived before God. Daniel's testimony comes out of how he lives and from his reaction to the circumstances in which he finds himself. These stories tell us a lot about the proper relationship between an individual and God.

§ God uses dreams to communicate with human beings, both the faithful and the nonbeliever.

§ For the truth of the dream to be revealed, a person must have realistic perspective on the universe. This perspective is that God is in control.

§ To be fully human means to be in proper relationship with God.

§ Public praise and confession are part of an individual's relationship to God. The community of faith and the world at large can learn of God through such confession and praise.

§ God uses both human beings and heavenly beings to bring about God's will for the world.

§ Individual lives as well as great historic events are under God's control.

§ Righteousness is required of God's servants even in the face of death.

§ Sin is bondage. Righteousness is true freedom.

§ Faithfulness is rewarded.

§ § § § § § §

Conclusions on Daniel 1–6

These are very personal, dramatic stories. They involve particular people in specific real-life situations. Yet, these particular people and circumstances reflect a wider and longer-range view of reality. Their stories always point the listener and the reader to God as the fundamental factor in all reality.

§ God is shown to be at work in individual lives and in the course of world events, though individuals are still free to choose between sin and righteousness.

§ Heaven and earth are related, and earthly events have their divine dimension. This dimension is God's will which is worked throughout heaven and earth.

§ God's people can be faithful to God and still thrive in an alien culture.

§ Daniel's exile and his position in Babylonia are used by God for good.

§ Human power is temporary and limited; God's power is eternal and without limit.

§ § § § § § §

Introduction to These Chapters

Chapters 7–9 of Daniel contain four vision reports.
With the vision in chapter 7 the focus of the book shifts
from Daniel's time in Babylon to future times in the
world at large. Chapters 1–6 center on people and events
from the Exile. Chapters 7–12 involve cosmic
principalities and powers as well.

Here is an outline of chapters 7–9.

I. Vision of Four Beasts (7:1-28)
  A. Daniel has a dream (7:1)
  B. The four beasts (7:2-8)
  C. The heavenly court (7:9-10)
  D. Judgment on the beasts (7:11-12)
  E. One like a son of man (7:13-14)
  F. The vision is interpreted (7:15-18)
  G. More about the fourth beast (7:19-22)
  H. Persecution and triumph (7:23-28)
II. Vision of the Ram and the He-Goat (8:1-27)
  A. Introduction (8:1-2)
  B. The ram (8:3-4)
  C. The he-goat (8:5-8)
  D. The destructive little horn (8:9-12)
  E. The sanctuary is desolate (8:13-14)
  F. A heavenly interpreter (8:15-19)
  G. More about the little horn (8:20-26)
  H. Conclusion (8:27)
III. Daniel's Prayer (9:1-27)
  A. The prayer (9:3-19)

B. Confession (9:4-6)

C. The case against Israel (9:7-14)

D. Gabriel answers Daniel's Prayer (9:20-27)

Vision of Four Beasts (7:1-28)

This vision, like the vision in Daniel 2, tells of four great kingdoms which have dominion on earth. These kingdoms will fall and be replaced by God's everlasting kingdom. No timetable is given for this event, but the message is clear that human power is limited and is subject to God's will.

Daniel Has a Dream (7:1)

Belshazzar's first year as king was approximately 550/549 B.C. His father, Nabonidus, was away from Babylon about ten years while traveling in the western regions of his empire.

Daniel's vision is no ordinary dream but is a revelation from God. In the vision Daniel is caught up in a cosmic drama in which the future of heaven and earth are symbolically acted out.

Verse 1 (also Daniel 10:1) was written by the editor of the book of Daniel as an introduction to this vision.

The Four Beasts (7:2-8)

The *four winds of heaven* are winds from all directions, from the four corners of the earth. The *great sea* is a vast ocean. The *four great beasts* are strange and terrifying symbols of power that come out of the chaotic waters. Images of such beasts have been found on both Babylonian and Assyrian monuments.

These four beasts represent four powerful kings and their great empires. None of these kings are named within the vision. However, just as with the kingdoms spoken of in chapter 2, these beasts have been identified with various historical kingdoms. There is disagreement among scholars as to which kingdom applies best to which beast.

The lion (verse 4) may correspond to the king of

Babylon. This beast represents brute power which is uncontrolled until the beast is humanized.

The second beast is like a bear which is perhaps standing on its hind legs, ready to attack. This beast may correspond to the king of Media or to the king of Media and Persia. Media was part of the Persian empire before Babylon fell in 539 B.C. This beast is given the power of conquest (*Arise, devour much flesh*).

The third beast may correspond to the king of Persia or to the king of Greece. Its four wings and four heads may represent its great dominion over the four corners of the earth. As with the first and second beasts, it is under the control of another force. This beast does not take its own dominion but is given dominion by God.

The fourth beast may correspond to the king of Greece or to the king of Rome. This beast is different from and more terrible than the others. Human kingdoms do not improve in this sequence, they grow more destructive. Further descriptions of this fourth beast are given in verses 19-21 and verses 23-25.

A *horn* generally represents strength and power. The horns are symbols from the animal world for this beast's tremendous power and influence. This little horn has eyes like a man and a mouth which speaks proud words, or speaks arrogantly.

The Heavenly Court (7:9-10)

Daniel sees God (the *ancient of days* [NIV] or *an ancient one* [NRSV]) and the heavenly hosts take their places in court to render a judgment against the beasts. God sits down on the chariot-throne (see also Ezekiel 1:15-28). Books of evidence are opened (see also Exodus 32:32-33) and a judgment is handed down.

Judgment on the Beasts (7:11-12)

The fourth beast is killed because of the *arrogant* (NRSV) or *boastful* (NIV) *words* spoken by the little horn. The other three beasts are not killed. Though the kingdoms they represent are not destroyed, their power is taken away.

The *period of time* (NIV) or *season and a time* (NRSV) is a length of time known only to God. Human history and time have not yet been replaced by God's kingdom, though God's judgment has begun. Just as with the kingdoms of the statue in chapter 2, these kingdoms symbolically exist side-by-side. One kingdom does not destroy or replace another in the sequence of the vision. Even after the fourth beast is killed, the other three live on.

These beasts may represent particular historical human kingdoms. They also may represent worldwide kingdoms and powerful human kings in general.

One Like a Son of Man (7:13-14)

One like a son of man (NIV) is *one like a human being* (NRSV). New Testament references by Jesus to the Son of man (for example, Matthew 19:28; Mark 13:26-27) reflect the same majesty and power given to him in Daniel. This one is like a human being but he shares God's limitless dominion. Clouds signal his coming (see Matthew 24:30-31; Revelation 1:7), just as clouds, fire, and wind are signals of God's presence.

The Vision Is Interpreted (7:15-18)

Daniel is worried by what he has seen of the fourth beast. A member of the heavenly court answers his questions.

The *four great beasts* are four kings of the earth.

The *Most High* is the *Ancient of Days* or *Ancient One*.

The *saints* (NIV) or *holy ones* (NRSV) are righteous believers who are called by God's name. These saints share in the kingdom which has been given to the *one like a son of man* or *like a human being* (verse 13).

More About the Fourth Beast (7:19-22)

Daniel describes the fourth beast in greater detail. These verses tell more of what happened in the vision before the fourth beast was killed (verse 11).

The king represented by the little horn fought against the saints and, for a while, had dominion over them. This king may correspond to the Greek ruler Antiochus IV who ruled Palestine from 175 B.C. to 164 B.C. He wanted to destroy Jewish faith and practice and to replace it with Greek religion and culture.

Persecution and Triumph (7:23-28)

The heavenly interpreter gives Daniel more information about the time of the fourth beast.

The last king of the fourth kingdom will blaspheme God and continually persecute God's people.

The *times* (NIV) or *sacred seasons* (NRSV) are religious festivals. The *law* is religious law by which the saints live.

A time may mean a year or it may mean a period of time known only to God (as in verse 12). This is a limited time, however, which is set by God.

All dominions (NRSV) or *all rulers* (NIV) (verse 27) is parallel to *all peoples, nations, and languages* (verse 14). Other earthly powers remain, but they are subject to the power of the saints and the son of man.

God's people did not receive such a kingdom as this when the Greek or the Roman empires collapsed. The Jewish saints did prevail over Antiochus IV in 164 B.C., but their political kingdom was not everlasting.

Jesus speaks of the coming of the Son of man. He also speaks of the final judgment in favor of God's saints as being in the future (see Matthew 16:27; 24:15, 30; 26:64; Mark 13:14).

There is evidence of this final kingdom in the coming of Christ, but it is not yet fully realized. This kingdom in Daniel 7 may refer to the kingdom of the saints at the Second Coming of Christ. In the vision, the future is enacted, and, for a time, the present and future coexist. The future is not yet fully realized in the earthly dimension, but it is already accomplished within the vision. Thus, Daniel's vision may be fulfilled in some respects but not in others.

Vision of the Ram and the He-Goat (8:1-27)

In approximately 550 B.C., during the reign of the Babylonian king Belshazzar, Daniel receives a vision concerning the kings of Media and Persia and the kings of Greece. Particular attention is given to a Greek king who desolates the sanctuary and persecutes the saints.

Introduction (8:1-2)

Daniel is in Babylon but is transported in this vision to Susa.

The Ram (8:3-4)

The ram, a symbol of strength, is the Median-Persian kingdom (see verse 20). The higher horn represents the kings of Persia who did as they pleased in conquest.

The He-Goat (8:5-8)

The goat *from the west* is a symbol of power and leadership (see also Ezekiel 34:17; 39:18). Goats typically lead the way when flocks of sheep and goats are pastured together. This goat represents the Greek empire. The *horn* probably represents Alexander the Great.

Alexander began his military campaign against the Persian empire in 334 B.C. and took control of Persia three years later. He died of fever at age 32, in 323 B.C. in Babylon. After his death, four of his generals divided his empire among them.

The Destructive Little Horn (8:9-12)

The little horn is a tyrant who seeks equality with God, the *Prince of the host.*

This little horn may correspond to Antiochus IV (175–164 B.C.). Antiochus was a descendant of one of Alexander's generals who took over part of the Greek empire, including Judah. Judah is *the glorious land.*

The *host of heaven* or *stars* may be the people of Israel.

The *regular burnt offering* (NRSV) or *daily sacrifice* (NIV) is the ritual of evening and morning sacrifices which are held in the Temple in Jerusalem. God's sanctuary is attacked as the little horn tries to make itself greater than God.

God's people are persecuted, sacrifices in the Temple are stopped, and God's truth is cast aside by the transgressor, the little horn.

The Sanctuary Is Desolate (8:13-14)

Two heavenly beings discuss a question which is probably also on Daniel's mind: "How long?"

The transgression or rebellion that causes desolation may refer to the worship of pagan gods within the Temple in Jerusalem. This would leave the Temple desolate or empty of God's presence (as in Ezekiel's vision in Ezekiel 8-11).

Evenings and mornings probably refers to the regular evening and morning sacrifices in the Temple. This would mean that it will be 1,150 days before the sanctuary is restored.

In 167 B.C., Antiochus IV was determined to have the Israelites live, think, and worship as Greeks. Under his rule, offerings to God in the Temple were outlawed for approximately three years. An altar to Zeus was set up over the altar of burnt offering within the Temple. Israelites were forbidden to practice their faith and were killed if they were caught with a Book of the Law (Genesis–Deuteronomy).

A Heavenly Interpreter (8:15-19)

Daniel is overcome in the presence of Gabriel, God's messenger. Gabriel addresses Daniel as *son of man,* meaning *human being.*

The *end* (verse 17) is related to the prophetic *latter days* when Israel's enemies will be destroyed and Israel will once again live in right relationship to God. The end of time in this vision also focuses on the restoration of Temple services (see verse 26).

Within the context of this vision, *the end* means particularly an end of *the wrath* (verse 19). The Hebrew word for wrath refers to the *wrath of God* which is aroused because of sin. The sin which arouses God's wrath in this case is the oppression of God's people by the little horn. Daniel sees and hears that this oppression has an appointed time to end.

More About the Little Horn (8:20-26)

Gabriel describes the king of the little horn more fully. This king will be harsh and insolent, though intelligent enough to prosper through deceit. He will be proud, self-centered, and cunning. Many people will die because of his power. He will even rise up against God (*the Prince of princes*).

This king will not win, however. By God's power, not human power, his reign of terror and blasphemy will end.

At one time during his reign, Antiochus IV had coins made which pictured him as the god Zeus. It is said that at the end of his life he was not mentally stable and that he died in 164 B.C. after falling from a roof.

The description of the king of the little horn fits Antiochus and his reign in many ways. This description could also apply to other leaders known in history and could apply to tyrants in general. Whatever ruthless leaders God's people may face, however, they are assured that God is in control and that tyranny will end.

Seal up the vision means to keep the vision a secret. Daniel's record of the vision must be guarded from misuse because the vision does not apply to the immediate future.

Conclusion (8:27)

This vision from God weighs heavily on Daniel. He continues his daily life in Babylon, but he is alarmed by what he has seen and heard. Though Daniel is wise and earnestly seeks God's revelation, he does not understand this vision.

Daniel's Prayer (9:1-27)

In approximately 605 B.C., the prophet Jeremiah told the people of Israel they could expect to serve the king of Babylon for seventy years because they had turned away from God (see Jeremiah 25:11-12). During the reign of King Zedekiah of Judah (597–587 B.C.) Jeremiah wrote a letter to the Israelite exile community in Babylon telling them to expect seventy years of punishment at the hands of the Babylonians (Jeremiah 29:10-14). He also urged them to make a home for themselves in Babylonia, to marry, have children, and to seek their welfare in Babylon's welfare (Jeremiah 29:4-9).

In the first year of King Darius, 538/539 B.C., Daniel reads a copy of Jeremiah's prophecies and sees that seventy years of punishment must pass before Jerusalem's restoration.

The Scripture in Jeremiah does not say from what point the seventy years are to be counted. From Jeremiah's prophecy in 605 B.C. (Jeremiah 25:11) to the defeat of Babylon by the Medes and Persians (539 B.C.) is sixty-six years. From 605 B.C. to the decree of Cyrus in 538 B.C. allowing the exiled Jews to return home (see Ezra 1:1-4) is sixty-seven years. From the destruction of Jerusalem and the Temple by Nebuchadnezzar in 587 B.C. to the dedication of the Second Temple in 516 B.C. (Ezra 6:14-15) is seventy-one years.

Seventy years may also be a symbolic number. The number seven and its multiples are used many times in the Old Testament, and, in general, they symbolize completeness, perfection, and consummation.

The Prayer (9:3-19)

In 539/538 B.C., Daniel goes to God in prayer on behalf of the people of Israel. He goes without food and he wears sackcloth and ashes as people do in mourning. This is a sign of Daniel's sincerity and of his penitence on behalf of Israel. Jerusalem and the Temple are still in ruins from the destruction of 587 B.C., and the people of Israel are scattered.

Daniel begins his prayer with an affirmation of faith in God's love and loyalty toward God's people. He goes on to confess Israel's sins which are in contrast to God's righteousness, justice, mercy, and forgiveness. He recalls God's mighty actions in the past on Israel's behalf and then asks for God's mercy and action for Israel and Jerusalem. Daniel bases his plea not on Israel's worthiness but on God's mercy.

An end to Israel's suffering has been announced by Jeremiah. Now Daniel claims that promise as well.

Confession (9:4-6)

The word of God is reliable and just. In contrast, the people of Israel have sinned against God and one another (*have sinned and done wrong*), have acted perversely (acted wickedly), and have rebelled against God's will. God's will is plain in the *commands* (NIV) or *commandments* (NRSV) (the principles of the law) and in the *ordinances* (NRSV) or *laws* (NIV) (the rules by which the commandments are applied to life).

The Case Against Israel (9:7-14)

Daniel continues to contrast Israel's confusion (literally, *shame*) and guilt with God's consistent mercy and justice.

The *curse(s) and oath* (NRSV) or *sworn judgments* (NIV) . . . *in the law of Moses* are found in Leviticus 26:14-39 and Deuteronomy 28:15-45. God warned Israel about the cost of disobedience to the covenant. Now God's word has been fulfilled. Daniel builds a case against Israel and then proclaims the prophetic "therefore": God has passed judgment and punished Israel.

A Plea for Deliverance (9:15-19)

Once Israel's guilt is confessed, Daniel pleads with God for mercy and makes a case for Israel's deliverance. He names God's saving acts of the past (verses 15-16*a*) and the vindication of God's name before the world (verses 16*b*-19) as reasons for God to act.

In biblical usage, a name is more than just identification for a person or for God. A name also reveals something of the nature and character of a person. Thus God's name must be honored and the people called by God's name must share in God's nature.

Daniel says that God may be regarded as powerless by other nations because the people, city, and Temple called by God's name are in ruins. God and Israel will be vindicated before the world when Jerusalem is restored.

Gabriel Answers Daniel's Prayer (9:20-27)

Gabriel comes to Daniel again to give him *insight* (NIV) or *wisdom and understanding* (NRSV) concerning Israel's future. The *word* (NRSV) or *answer* (NIV) which went forth is a word from God which brings a message from God and a revelation of God's will. This word also carries God's creative power. Daniel is to use this word to gain understanding of what is revealed to him.

Daniel's plea for the restoration of Israel is granted (verse 24), and then Gabriel tells Daniel when and how this will happen (verses 25-27).

Gabriel applies Jeremiah's prophecy farther into the future than just the end of the Babylonian Empire (see Jeremiah 25:11). According to Gabriel, seventy weeks of years, or 490 years, will pass before sin is ended and atonement made. Leviticus 25:1-12 says that *seven weeks* (or *sabbaths*, NIV) *of years* (forty-nine years) are counted before the fiftieth year which is a jubilee, a year of liberty. The jubilee year is holy and is a time when each person will return to his property . . . and his family (Leviticus 25:10).

After 490 years, Israel will be forgiven and liberated. An age of eternal righteousness will begin. Then Daniel's (and Jeremiah's) vision will be sealed, that is, confirmed.

The *most holy place* or *most holy one* may be the holy of holies in the Temple, or it may be the anointed one who is to come (verse 25).

Many different interpretations have been given for verses 25-27, and various identities have been given to the people and times mentioned here. Some of these interpretations apply to the years between Daniel's time and our time, and some apply to our future.

Just as God's people have known more than one tyrant like the one described in Daniel 7, so also have they known (and will know) more than one desolator (verse 27). Gabriel's word to Daniel concerning Jeremiah's prophecy shows that prophecies may apply to more than one time and in more than one dimension. Jeremiah declared that seventy years would pass before Babylon would be punished and the exiles allowed to return home. This punishment has been accomplished, and the exiles are about to be free to go home. In this sense, Jeremiah's prophecy is fulfilled. Gabriel, however, shows Daniel how this prophecy also applies to the distant future.

The *issuing of the decree* (NIV) or *the time that the word went out* (NRSV) (verse 25) may have been in 587 B.C. after the first Temple was destroyed. After 587 B.C. both Ezekiel (Ezekiel 36:8-11) and Jeremiah (Jeremiah 29:10; 31:23-34) spoke of Jerusalem's restoration.

The going forth of the word may also have been in 538 B.C. when King Cyrus of Persia decreed that the Temple was to be restored and that the captive Israelites could return home.

The work to fully restore Jerusalem was not begun until the time of Nehemiah in 445 B.C.

An anointed one, a prince is a leader. This may be King Cyrus, who issued his decree in 538 B.C., forty-nine years (*seven sevens*) after the Temple was destroyed in 587 B.C.

This leader might be Zerubbabel, or it might be Jeshua who led in the rebuilding of the Temple (520–516 B.C.).

Jerusalem will be rebuilt and fortified for 434 days (*sixty-two weeks* [NRSV] or *sixty-two sevens* [NIV]). Troubled times may refer to the domination of Judah by the Persians and Greeks (and Romans?). This time may also point to the religious and moral problems the people of Israel faced in Judah after the Exile (see Ezra and Nehemiah).

The *anointed one* (verse 26) may refer to Onias III, who was the High Priest in the Temple until he was driven from office by the Greek king Antiochus IV. Onias was killed in 171 B.C. The prince or ruler who is to come may correspond to Antiochus IV. The *people of the prince* (NRSV) or *ruler* (NIV) are his army. Antiochus' forces brought death and destruction to Jerusalem. They did not, however, completely destroy the Temple or the city. Roman forces under the general Titus destroyed Jerusalem and the Temple in A.D. 70.

The end (NIV) or *its* (NRSV) may also mean *his*, referring to the prince. The flood may be a figure of speech for divine punishiment (see also Nahum 1:8).

Though an end will come, God's people must endure war and desolations during the last week of the seventy weeks.

Verse 27 deals with the last week of desolations. On the basis of his strength, the prince will be in alliance with many people. Sacrifices and offerings in the Temple will stop for half of this final week.

The exact meaning of *the wing of the temple* (NIV: Alluded to in *place* in NRSV) is not clear. The wing may be the top of the Temple or perhaps the corner of the altar. The abomination may refer to the altar to Zeus which was set up on top of the altar of burnt offering in the Temple.

The *abomination that causes desolation* (NIV) or the *abomination that desolates* (NRSV) may be someone who comes after the prince. Whoever this desolator is, his end has been established by God. God's destruction, overflowing with righteousness (Isaiah 10:22), will be poured out against the desolator of God's people.

The people and times of this vision cannot be

completely identified. As we have seen, the numbers given may be symbolic rather than strictly chronological. The stages in human history defined here serve as guides for Daniel and his readers. These guides help us understand the past and point our way into the future, but they do not explain everything. These revelations help us recognize God's plan for the world as it unfolds.

The Gospel writers take up these guides to reveal more about the future. Jesus refers to the abomination of desolation (compare Daniel 8:13; 9:27; 11:31 with the "desolating sacrilege" of Matthew 24:25-31; Mark 13:14-27) as heralding the destruction of the Temple. The Romans destroyed the Temple and the city in A.D. 70.

Jesus goes on to talk about the coming of the Son of Man and the glory that is to follow the end of the desolations. He points to a future relevance of Daniel's visions (compare Matthew 24:29-31; Luke 21:27; Daniel 7:13-14).

Though the message of the vision in Daniel 9 may have been fulfilled in times past, it may still apply to other phases in God's plan for the world.

§ § § § § § §

The Message of Daniel 7–9

The symbols and message of Daniel 7–9 are not easily understood. Attempts to pin down every reference will end in frustration. Yet, visions are granted for the benefit of the community of faith. What then can we learn from this material that does not yield its secrets easily?

§ God is in control of history and of human destiny. No one lives outside of God's dominion.

§ God has a plan for history in which righteousness will overcome sin.

§ God's people will suffer but will be victorious in the end. They will share in God's coming kingdom.

§ The future may be known to some extent, but the final timetable is in God's hands.

§ A well-lived, well-disciplined life of faith which includes prayer brings ultimate rewards.

§ § § § § § §

Introduction to These Chapters

Chapters 10–12 tell of a vision *for days yet to come*
which comes to Daniel in approximately 535 B.C. Daniel
10:1–11:1 introduces the vision and Daniel's heavenly
messenger. Daniel 11:2–12:4 reports the message of the
vision. Daniel 12:5-13 concludes the vision and gives a
personal message for Daniel concerning his future.

Here is an outline of these chapters.

I. Vision by the Great River (10:1–11:1)
   A. Daniel in mourning (10:2-3)
   B. Daniel sees the vision (10:4-9)
   C. Daniel is strengthened (10:10-17)
   D. Heavenly conflict (10:18–11:1)
II. Revelation of the Future (11:2-45)
   A. Kings of Persia and Greece (11:2-4)
   B. The north and the south (11:5-6)
   C. The south against the north (11:7-9)
   D. The north victorious (11:10-16)
   E. The king of the north meets defeat (11:17-19)
   F. The king of a few days (11:20)
   G. A contemptible person (11:21-24)
   H. The appointed end is yet to come (11:25-28)
   I. Jerusalem suffers (11:29-31)
   J. Jewish revolt (11:32-35)
   K. According to God's will (11:36-39)
   L. The end of the tyrant (11:40-45)
III. The Time of the End (12:1-13)
   A. Deliverance from a time of trouble (12:1)

B. Resurrection of the dead (12:2-3)
C. The vision is sealed (12:4)
D. How long? (12:5-7)
E. What shall be the issue? (12:8-10)
F. Days of the appointed end (12:11-12)
G. Daniel's place at the end of days (12:13)

Vision by the Great River (10:1–11:1)

The Hebrew in the middle of verse 1 is difficult to translate. The NRSV says, *And the word was true, and it was a great conflict.* The NIV says, *Its message was true and it concerned a great war.*

Daniel in Mourning (10:2-3)

Daniel may have been in mourning because of difficulties the Jews in Jerusalem were having in rebuilding the Temple (see Ezra 5:14-16). As a sign of mourning, Daniel does not anoint himself with oil nor does he eat any *choice* (NIV) or *rich* (NRSV) *food*. He may also have been seeking further understanding of the word he had received concerning the future (see verse 12).

Daniel Sees the Vision (10:4-9)

The *first month* is the month of Nisan (our March/April). Daniel sees a heavenly being, whose appearance is dazzling. At the sight, Daniel's vigor and strength are drained and he lapses into unconsciousness.

Daniel Is Strengthened (10:10-17)

The messenger must strengthen Daniel three times (see verses 16 and 18) before Daniel can face the glory of heaven which is reflected in the man and in his message. Such a revelation cannot be taken lightly, nor does it come without personal cost.

The *prince* of Persia is the patron angel of Persia, and Michael is the patron angel of Israel (see Daniel 12:1). The conflict between these angels in heaven mirrors the conflicts between peoples on earth.

The prince of Persia tries to keep the messenger from coming to Daniel to announce the defeat of Persia (see verse 20; 11:2-3) because the announcement of God's word is part of its accomplishment.

The *end of days* (NRSV) are days *in the future* (NIV); they are days yet to come. These days lead up to the time of the end (see also Daniel 8:17; 11:35, 40; 12:4, 9).

Heavenly Conflict (10:8–11:1)

This messenger is also a patron angel who fights in the heavenly wars. He championed the cause of Darius the Mede, who acted within God's will in defeating Babylon and in supporting the Jews (see Daniel 6:25-28). This messenger angel also will fight along with Michael on behalf of God's people against the angels of Persia and Greece.

What happens on earth is reflected in heaven. This heavenly reality, which is not usually visible to human beings (except see Daniel 7), affects human history.

The *book of the truth* is God's book in which human destiny is recorded (see also Psalm 40:7; Malachi 3:16).

Revelation of the Future (11:2-45)

Many of the details in this vision report can be identified from other historical documents. However, as we have seen in other visions in Daniel, such identification does not necessarily explain the whole meaning of the text. Nor does historical identification eliminate other possible applications of the text. Some of the signs and references to the future within the vision may be fulfilled in our past and yet hold the promise of further relevance in our future.

These texts also treat time in more than one way. There is time as we know it, chronological or historical time, and there is time from God's eternal perspective. God's time does not necessarily go according to our time.

Human beings live in chronological or "event-full" time and also live in God's time (though we may not be aware of it). God's time takes a longer view of reality and includes qualities and meanings which may not be easily seen. We must search for this larger reality and seek God's guidance in it just as Daniel did.

Daniel teaches us that "event-full" time (called *chronos* in Greek) leads to a "fullness" of time (called *kairos* in Greek). This fullness of time is a decisive moment in time. It is to such a moment that the events of Daniel 11–12 lead. At this decisive moment God's kingdom will be fully realized and God's people will live in right relationship to God and to one another.

Kings of Persia and Greece (11:2-4)

Three more kings . . . and a *fourth* may be a figure of speech which symbolizes all of Persia's rulers. During Persia's 200 years in power there were ten kings.

Alexander the Great of Greece (the *mighty* [NIV] or *warrior* [NRSV] king) defeated the Persians in 331 B.C. Eventually, his empire stretched from the Adriatic Sea to India. He died at the height of his power in 332 B.C. and four of his generals divided his empire among them. His two sons were murdered thirteen years later.

The North and the South (11:5-6)

Verses 5-20 deal with the struggles for power between the rulers of the divided Greek empire.

The *south* is Egypt which was ruled by Ptolemy I (323–285 B.C.). Judah was included in his kingdom.

One of his princes was Seleucus I (312–281 B.C.), also one of Alexander's generals. He was the *king of the north* whose kingdom centered in Syria.

After some years is in approximately 250 B.C. Ptolemy II of Egypt gave his daughter, Bernice, in marriage to Antiochus II of Syria, but the alliance did not last. Antiochus, Bernice, and their son were killed by Laodice, Antiochus' former wife, so that her son, Seleucus II, could be king of Syria.

The South Against the North (11:7-9)

The *branch* is Bernice's brother, Ptolemy III (247–221 B.C.). In revenge for his sister's death, he plundered the northern capital and overran the territory of Seleucus II as far as Babylon. Seleucus's army attacked Egypt in 242 B.C. but was defeated.

The North Victorious (11:10-16)

In 198 B.C., Antiochus III (then the king of the north) defeated Egyptian forces near the headwaters of the Jordan River. Judah then came under Syrian rule.

The *violent men* (NIV) or *lawless among your people* (NRSV) were Jewish revolutionaries who took up arms against their Egyptian overlords. They wanted to restore Israel as an independent nation, but the time was not right. Many of the Jews suffered during the warfare between Egypt and Syria. They welcomed the rule of Antiochus III and the peace it brought.

The *beautiful land* is Judah.

The King of the North Meets Defeat (11:17-19)

Anciochus III's daughter married Ptolemy V of Egypt as part of Antiochus' plan to control Egypt, but the plan failed.

Antiochus turned his forces toward the coastlands of the Mediterranean. In doing so he met the growing military might of Rome. *A commander* is Lucius Scipio, the Roman commander who stopped Antiochus' advance and forced him to retreat to Syria as well as to pay tribute to Rome. Thus, the power of Rome was already beginning to be felt in Palestine.

The King of a Few Days (11:20)

Seleucus IV (187–175 B.C.) sent one of his officers to get money from the Temple treasury in Jerusalem to help pay his tribute to Rome.

A few days (NRSV) or *years* (NIV) refers to the short reign of this king. Seleucus IV was king for twelve years before his assassination in 175 B.C. As we apply the vision in verse 20 to him, we must admit the difficulties involved in coordinating the times given in Daniel with the actual dates of historical events. The revelations in Daniel have a heavenly and eternal perspective as well as an earthly perspective. Within this large view of God's redemptive purposes, twelve years does seem as a few days or years.

A Contemptible Person (11:21-24)

By crafty promises and intrigues Antiochus IV (175–164 B.C.), a *contemptible person*, won the throne of his dead brother.

The *prince of the covenant* may be the high priest of the Temple, Onias III. Antiochus was a deceitful schemer who made or broke alliances as it suited his needs. He accepted a bribe from Joshua, Onias's brother, and made him high priest. After three years Antiochus got rid of Joshua in favor of Menelaus, who paid even more money for the office.

These Jews and others were part of the *few people* (NIV) or *small party* (NRSV) who cooperated with Antiochus and supported his introduction of Greek religion and culture into Judah.

The Appointed End Is Yet to Come (11:25-28)

According to the vision, the political and military plots of the kings of the north and south will not work out. The appointed time for the end of all this has not yet come.

The king of the north took out his frustration on Jerusalem by plundering the Temple and persecuting the faithful Jews.

Notice the phrase *he shall work his will* (NRSV) or *take action against it* (NIV). This phrase appears four times in chapter 11 (verses 3, 16, 28, 36). This is said of three different kings who are strong militarily and who rule over the people of Israel. The repetition indicates an important characteristic of rulers at many times in history. These rulers set out to act according to their own self-interest rather than according to God's will. Though we may see that particular Greek kings fulfill these descriptions given in Daniel 11, they also represent a type of oppressor that God's people have known in many ages and may know in years to come.

Jerusalem Suffers (11:29-31)

Antiochus IV again attacked Egypt but Roman forces from Cyprus (called *Kittim*) stopped his advance and sent him in humiliation back to Syria. He vented his anger on Jerusalem. Many Jews were killed, Jerusalem's walls were broken down, and Greek forces were stationed there.

Those who forsake the holy covenant are Jews who supported Antiochus' efforts to bring Jews and their God into Greek culture and religion.

The *abomination* may be the altar or idol to Zeus which was set up in the Temple. This made the Temple desolate of God's presence.

Jewish Revolt (11:32-35)

The *wise* are those who know their God, who lead others to wisdom, and who will die rather than abandon their faith. They understand that God and God's people will be victorious.

The *little help* may refer to the open revolt against Antiochus which broke out in 167 B.C. This revolt was led by Judas Maccabeus and his family. The revolt came to be called the Maccabean Revolution.

The faithful who die purify themselves and the community. Their sacrifice paves the way for the appointed end of tribulation.

According to God's Will (11:36-39)

Trying to be like God is a sin to which all human beings are subject (see, for example, Genesis 3:5), but this ruler carried it to an extreme.

Antiochus IV claimed to be divine and issued coins which said *of king Antiochus, god manifest.*

The End of the Tyrant (11:40-45)

The *end* is the end of the time allowed by God for this cruel king to reign. This end may also refer to the end of the age when, in the fullness of time, God's kingdom fills the earth and replaces the kingdoms of earthly rulers.

The historical details about this last conflict between the kings of the north and south are not known. The details given in the vision do not coordinate with what is known from other sources about the end of Antiochus's reign. Some scholars believe that this section identifies the time when Daniel was written—in approximately 165 B.C. between the "history" the writer knew in Daniel 1:1–11:39 and the "predictions" about Antiochus IV in 11:40-45. Other scholars believe that Daniel was written as prophecy. Some of this prophecy would apply to Antiochus and some would apply to other leaders and circumstances both in the past and in the future.

In 166 B.C. Antiochus had to deal with rebellion in Judah as well as in other parts of his kingdom. His forces were divided, and in 165 B.C. Jewish rebels took control of Judah. The Temple was cleansed and rededicated in December 165/164 B.C. The Feast of Hanukkah has been celebrated ever since in honor of this joyous event.

The *beautiful land* is Judah. The *palatial* (NRSV) or *royal* (NIV) *tents* are the royal headquarters on the field of battle. The sea(s) is the Mediterranean, and the *beautiful holy mountain* is Mount Zion in Jerusalem.

Chapter 11 testifies that the proud and willful tyrants of human history may have their day, but they always fall before the will of God.

The Time of the End (12:1-13)

With this chapter the vision and the book come to an end. We are given a glimpse of the end of Daniel's life and assurance of life after death for Daniel and for those who remain faithful to God.

Deliverance from a Time of Trouble (12:1)

Michael fights along with the angel messenger against the princes of Persia and Greece. He then comes to stand by God's people and rescue them from the great tribulation in which they are caught.

The *book* records the names of God's faithful (see also Exodus 32:32-33; Revelation 3:5).

Resurrection of the Dead (12:2-3)

The dead (those *who sleep in the dust*) will be awakened to new life. *Many* (NRSV) may mean *all* or *multitudes* (NIV), those who have died before this end time. Those who are faithful to God awaken to everlasting life. This is not just a life which is unending. It is also a life of great reward and fulfillment.

In contrast, those who are not faithful to God awaken to unending disgrace and aversion. Behind the meaning of *contempt* is the idea that to be contemptible is to be accounted as nothing. For the unfaithful, there is to be only emptiness with no true life at all.

This part of the vision applies to the time of Antiochus IV in a symbolic sense. After years of desolation the people of Israel were delivered to new life under Jewish rulers. This kingdom lasted until 63 B.C. when Rome took over Palestine.

This part of the vision may also apply to the future at *the end* of this age and at the beginning of God's kingdom on earth (see also John 5:28-29; Revelation 20:12-13).

Those who are wise is a reference to those who know God's truth, who live by this truth, and who teach others about this truth. These persons reflect God's radiant light of truth.

The Vision Is Sealed (12:4)

Daniel is to put away the record of what he has seen and heard (see also Daniel 8:26). To *seal* may mean to confirm, and to *close up* (NIV: translated as *keep the words secret* in the NRSV) may be symbolic of the fact that the end is fixed or confirmed by God. As we know, this record has not been hidden until the final end of all things.

In the meantime, people will continue to look far and wide for truth. Knowledge of God's truth will increase, in part because the wise will teach others and be an example to others to keep the faith.

How Long? (12:5-7)

A time of questions and answers ends the vision with two more heavenly beings coming to testify to the truth of what Daniel has heard.

The first messenger raises his hands as a sign to call heaven to witness to the truth of his answer. He swears by God (*him who lives forever*) that the end will be for *a time, two times, and a half a time* (NRSV) or *for a time, times and half a time* (NIV). This may be three and one-half years or it may be a time known only to God. A sign that the end is near will be the breaking of the power of God's people and their helplessness before their enemies.

What Shall Be the Issue? (12:8-10)

Despite his years of experience with revelations from God and his wisdom, Daniel does not understand what the outcome of all these events will be. Daniel is told to live his life in trust. He can live in trust because he has been assured that the end and the outcome of the end are in God's hands and are assured.

Those who are purified and refined may be those who will die in the fight for righteousness.

The wicked will continue in their sin because they do not understand the true significance of what is happening in the world. The wise, however, do understand. They see that God's will and power are directing and shaping the course of human history.

Days of the Appointed End (12:11-12)

In verse 11, the messenger returns to the issue of Temple desecration. One thousand two hundred and ninety days is approximately three and one-half years. This is close to the length of time during which Antiochus IV took over the Temple and set up his own altar there. This also approximates the one-half week of Daniel 9:27 when sacrifice and offering shall cease during the last week of the *seventy weeks of years* (NRSV) or *sabbaths* (NIV).

One thousand three hundred thirty-five days is about three and seven-tenths years. These days may complete the last one-half week of the seventy weeks of years. Those who continue in righteousness through these days to the end will be blessed and happy. They will see the vindication promised by God.

Daniel's Place at the End of Days (12:13)

Daniel will rest in death until the end of the days decreed by God. Then Daniel will rise with the others who *sleep in the dust* (verse 2) to his proper destiny among those blessed with everlasting life.

Daniel is told to go on about his life. He will not live to see the fulfillment of all that has been revealed to him, but he will awaken into God's kingdom.

Thus, Daniel's life and the book of Daniel end with a view into the future, a future that is determined by God.

§ § § § § § §

The Message of Daniel 10–12

Daniel 10–12 deals with history, people, and time in ways that are not easily interpreted. We may not fully understand the outcome of all we have read. We will miss great value in the text, however, if we only try to figure out how to match the prophecy with past or future events and times. The meaning of these texts and the motivation which produced them must not be overlooked.

Daniel was written, in part, so that we who came after Daniel would know more of God through him. Daniel requires us to remember our past, to know to what authority we must ultimately answer, and to allow the truth of the past to guide us into the future.

At the end of chapter 12 Daniel is told to go on with his life in trust. What do these chapters tell us about going on with our lives?

§ We must trust in God and have confidence in the final outcome of God's plan for the world.

§ We must be disciplined in the laws and practice of our faith.

§ We must maintain an openness to God's revelation.

§ We must witness to our experience of God's truth.

What does Jesus say about going on with our lives (for example, in Matthew 24–25; Mark 13)?

§ We must be ready for the end but not preoccupied with it.

§ We must witness to the gospel.

§ We must spend time in acts of charity.

§ We must persist in our duty even if the Master does not come at the appointed time.

§ § § § § § §

Glossary of Terms

Abomination: Anything that is ritually or ethically offensive to God and to God's people.

Akkadian: People living in the region between the Tigris and Euphrates Rivers before the Babylonians. The Babylonian language is an Akkadian dialect.

Amasis: Pharaoh who took the Egyptian throne from Pharaoh Hophra in 569 B.C.

Ammonites: A Semitic people living in Ammon, a territory in the Transjordan (land east of the Jordan River). Ammon was Israelite territory under King David.

Amorites: A Semitic people living in parts of Canaan and the Transjordan. Jerusalem was probably an Amorite town before the Israelites settled there.

Antiochus IV: Greek tyrant who ruled Syria and Palestine (175-164 B.C.) and who persecuted the Jews.

Arabah: The region of Israel running from the lower end of the Sea of Galilee, including the Jordan Valley and the Dead Sea, on to the Gulf of Aqabah.

Arabia: From a word meaning *desert* or *steppe,* a large peninsula in southwest Asia. In Ezekiel 27:21, it is a collective name for the people of this area. In Ezekiel 30:5 it indicates *mingled people.*

Aramaic: A term used to indicate a group of Semitic dialects which are closely related to Hebrew.

Arvad: An island city-state in northern Syria.

Asher: One of the twelve tribes of Israel, descended from the eighth son of Jacob.

Assyria: A civilization which, along with Babylonia, flourished in the area of Mesopotamia from approximately 2500-2000 B.C. to its defeat by Babylonia in approximately 612 B.C. Assyria took control of the Northern Kingdom (Israel) in 722 or 721 B.C.

Astarte: A Canaanite fertility goddess.

Atonement: Has the general meaning of *to be at one.* In the Old Testament, used in the sense of removing the effects of sin. Sacrifice is a means of removing the barrier between God and the people that is caused by sin. Sin is forgiven, the barrier removed, and God and people are at one.

Azariah: Hebrew name of Abednego, Daniel's friend.

Baal-Meon: A city in northern Moab.

Babylon: Empire which replaced Assyria as the dominant Mesopotamian civilization in 612 B.C. until its absorption by Persia in 539 B.C. Babylonia took control of the Southern Kingdom (Judah) in 598 B.C.

Bamah: High place; term used in relation to places of worship on natural or constructed hills.

Bashan: Region east and northeast of the Sea of Galilee and east of the Jordan River; it was well adapted to growing wheat and cattle and was famous for its groves of oak trees; was taken by the Israelites from the Amorites.

Bath: A liquid measuring unit; approximately five and one-half gallons.

Belshazzar: Son and co-ruler of Nabonidus who was the last king of the Babylonian empire (556-539 B.C.).

Benjamin: One of the twelve tribes of Israel, descended from a son of Jacob and Rachel.

Berothah: Place on the northern border of Ezekiel's ideal Israel.

Beth-Jeshimoth: A city in Moab.

Beth-Togarmah: Means *House of Togarmah*; a region in Asia Minor once part of the Assyrian Empire.

Blasphemy: Slandering, reproaching, cursing, or showing contempt for God or for something sacred; also, claiming divine qualities for oneself.

Byword: A sharp saying, curse, or taunt; also a proverbial object of scorn or derision.

Canaanites: The people occupying the land of Canaan (approximately the area of Palestine west of the Jordan River and part of Syria) at the time of the Israelite invasion under Joshua.

Canneh: Alternate form of Calneh, a city in the Babylonian Empire.

Cappadocia: A highland province in the territory of eastern Asia Minor.

Carchemish: Capital of the Hittite kingdom; Nebuchadnezzar defeated Pharaoh Neco here in 605 B.C.

Censer: A portable ladle or shovel for carrying live coals and for burning incense.

Chaldeans: Chaldea and Chaldeans were a region and a tribal group in southern Babylonia; during the time of Nebuchadnezzar's reign, *Chaldean* came to mean the same thing as *Babylonian.*

Chebar: A river which was a branch of the Euphrates River. There Ezekiel received his first vision.

Cherethites: People from the area of the Aegean Sea who settled on the coast of Palestine and became part of King David's mercenary army; they are associated with the Philistines.

Cherubim: Winged creatures who are angelic and spiritual beings.

Chilmad: A place in Assyria, near modern Baghdad.

Covenant: A solemn promise between two partners which is sealed with an oath and/or a symbolic action. The basic terms of God's covenant with Israel are found in the Ten Commandments (see Exodus 20:1-17; Deuteronomy 5:1-21).

Cubit: A unit for measuring length; approximately 18 inches, from elbow to fingertip.

Cyprus: Also called Kittim; an island in the Mediterranean Sea approximately forty miles from Asia Minor and sixty miles from Syria; famous for its copper.

Damascus: A city in Syria northeast of the Sea of Galilee, in an oasis watered by rivers and canals; an important center of commerce and religion.

Dan: One of the twelve tribes of Israel; descended from the fifth son of Jacob; also, the northernmost city and territory in Israel.

Darius the Mede: Named in Daniel 5:30 as ruler of the territory of Babylon after Babylon's defeat by the Medes and Persians in 539 B.C. and before the reign of Cyrus of Persia (see Daniel 6:28). His name and identity are not known outside of Scripture.

Dedan: Perhaps a settlement of Dedanites living in Edom; Dedanites were an important commercial and trading people who lived in northwest Arabia to the southeast of the territory of Edom.

Divination: The art of identifying the will and intentions of the gods, practiced by diviners; the Babylonians were the first group of people to develop this art to an almost scientific discipline.

Edom: The land and people to the south and east of Judah; the territory was named after a red rock and called the *red region.*

Egypt: A land in northwest Africa along the Nile River; one of the earliest and most powerful civilizations of the ancient Near East.

Elam: A region east of the Euphrates-Tigris Rivers on the slopes of the Iranian plateau. Susa was the capital of this region.

Elders: Grown men who are leaders in their clan, tribe, or community; they represent and maintain the community's customs and laws.

Elishah: An island, perhaps Cyprus.

En-Eglaim: A settlement on the northwest coast of the Dead Sea.

En-Gedi: An oasis on the west side of the Dead Sea.

Ephah: A unit of dry measure; approximately three-eighths to two-thirds of a bushel.

Ephraim: One of the twelve tribes of Israel, descended from the younger son of Joseph; also, later became a name for the people of Israel.

Ethiopia: The ancient name for the territory south of Egypt, approximately the area of present-day Sudan; also called Cush.

Euphrates: The largest river in western Asia, along with the Tigris; a major river of Mesopotamia.

Gad: One of the twelve tribes of Israel, descended from the seventh son of Jacob; also the name of settled land east of the Jordan and west of Ammon.

Gamad: A city in Syria.

Gebal: A Phoenician port city, center of trade and shipbuilding.

Gedaliah: Israelite governor of Judah under Babylonian rule, 587-582 B.C.

Gilead: The name of a territory, a tribe, and possibly a city located east of the Jordan River; it was famous for its medicinal balm.

Gog: Named in Ezekiel 39 as the leader of evil forces which will rise against the restored Israel; this leader's name and identity are not known outside of Scripture.

Gomer: Eldest son of Japheth and father of a people from a territory in what is now southern Russia.

Hamonah: City where Gog's forces will be destroyed.

Hamon Gog: Means *multitude of Gog*; a valley in the territory of the Transjordan where the dead of Gog's armies will be buried.

Hananiah: The Hebrew name of Shadrach, one of Daniel's three friends.

Haran: A commercial city in northern Mesopotamia.

Hauran: A region east of the Jordan River and the Sea of Galilee which marks the northeast limit of Ezekiel's ideal Israel.

Hazar-Enon: A city on the frontier between Palestine and Hamath in Syria.

Hazar-Hatticon: Probably the same place as Hazar-enon (see above).

Helbon: A city northwest of Damascus, famous for its wine production.

Helech: Possibly a country in southeast Asia Minor.

Hethlon: A city located on the northern border of Ezekiel's ideal Israel.

High places: Canaanite sanctuaries, either open-air or roofed, which were on high hills.

Hin: A unit of liquid measure that equals approximately one gallon.

Hittites: An Indo-European people who were a great power in Asia Minor from approximately 1650-1200 B.C.; later centers of their power were in the city of Hamath and in northern Syria.

Homer: A unit of dry measure that equals approximately 3-6 bushels.

Hophra: Pharaoh of Egypt, 588-569 B.C.

Horns of the altar: Projections sticking up from the top four corners of the Temple altar.

Incense: Compounds of gums and spices intended to be burned, or the perfume from such burning.

Israel: Israel, also called Jacob, was the son of Isaac and Rebekah; the *house of Israel* or *house of Jacob* means his descendants, the people of Israel; also the name of the Northern Kingdom which was formed when Solomon's sons divided his kingdom into Israel and Judah (also called the Southern Kingdom).

Issachar: One of the twelve tribes of Israel, descended from the ninth son of Jacob and Leah.

Javan: Either Greece/Asia Minor or a Greek colony or Arab tribe in Arabia.

Jehoiachin: Also called Jeconiah and Coniah, king of Judah (598-597 B.C.), carried into exile by Nebuchadnezzar.

Jehoiakim: King of Judah (609-597 B.C.), son of Josiah and brother of Jehoahaz.

Judah: One of the twelve tribes of Israel, descended from the fourth son of Jacob and Leah; also, the Southern Kingdom (see "Israel").

Kedar: An Arab tribe; also, an area east and southeast of Israel, part of present-day Jordan and Saudi Arabia.

Kiriathaim: A city in Moab.

Koa: Exact identity unknown, perhaps Aramean mercenaries in the army of Babylon.

Lebanon: A mountain range running parallel to the eastern Mediterranean coast; also the name of the adjacent coastlands; populated by Canaanites and the homeland of the Phoenicians.

Levi: One of the twelve tribes of Israel, descended from the third son of Jacob and Leah; also, Levites were a rank of priests set apart for service in the sanctuary.

Leviathan: A great sea monster or dragon; symbol of the forces of chaos and evil.

Libya: Area along the north African coast of the Mediterranean Sea which is just west of Egypt.

Lud: The son of Shem; also, the plural form (*Ludim*) may indicate two groups of people, one group living in Asia Minor and the other in North Africa.

Magog: The kingdom of Gog; represents any kingdom which challenges God's rule.

Manasseh: One of the twelve tribes of Israel, descended from the first son of Joseph.

Medes: People of the kingdom of Media, a territory in northwestern Iran which was first settled in 1400-1000 B.C.; became a province of the Persian Empire in approximately 549 B.C.

Memphis: Chief city of Lower (northern) Egypt.

Meribath-Kadesh: A place in the Wilderness of Zin in Kadesh at the southern border of Canaan and the western border of Edom.

Meshech: A people and country in Asia Minor, famous for their metal working; the land and subjects of Gog according to Ezekiel 39:1.

Mesopotamia: The land between the Tigris and Euphrates rivers, now in modern Iraq.

Migdol: A fortress in northern Egypt.

Mishael: The Hebrew name of Meshach, one of Daniel's three friends.

Moab: A area east of the Dead Sea and south of the Jordan River.

Nabonidus: The last king of the Babylonian Empire (from 556-539 B.C.).

Nabopolassar: King of Babylon (626-605 B.C.) and father of Nebuchadnezzar.

Naphtali: One of the twelve tribes of Israel, descended from the sixth son of Jacob.

Nebuchadnezzar/Nebuchadrezzar: King of Babylon (605-562 B.C.), conquered Judah and took thousands of Israelites into captivity.

Negeb: A dry region in southern Canaan which runs from the Sinai Peninsula to the Dead Sea; the name sometimes means *south.*

Nisan: The first month of the year in the Hebrew calendar, approximately March/April.

Pathros: Upper (southern) Egypt.

Pekod: Aramean tribe living along the Tigris River.

Pelusium: An important fortress town on Egypt's northern frontier.

Persia: A great empire in the ancient Near East from 550 B.C. to 330 B.C.; at its height it stretched from Greece eastward to India and was centered in what is now Iran.

Philistia: The fertile southern coastal plain of Palestine; the Philistines were Sea Peoples who settled along the coast in 1200 B.C. They were fierce fighters and were often at war with Israel.

Phoenicia: A group of city-states on the Mediterranean coast in what is now Lebanon; the Phoenicians were great seafarers, explorers, and traders who thrived from approximately 1200 to 146 B.C.

Pibeseth: A city in the Nile Delta.

Prefect: A governor or person appointed to a position of authority and command.

Ptolemy: The name of all male Egyptian rulers from the time of Alexander the Great (approximately 323 B.C.) until the time of the Roman Empire (approximately 80 B.C.).

Put: The third son of Ham; also a region in northern Africa, probably in Libya.

Raamah: A trading city in southwest Arabia.

Rabbah: An Israelite town in the hills west of Jerusalem; also, a city which was the capital of Ammon (also called Rabbah-ammon), now Amman, Jordan.

Reuben: One of the twelve tribes of Israel, descended from the first son of Jacob and Leah.

Rhodes: A Greek island and city in the southeast portion of the Aegean Sea.

Riblah: An ancient Syrian town north of Damascus; the military highways of Egypt and Mesopotamia crossed at this location.

Sackcloth: A garment made of goat's hair or camel's hair that was often worn as a symbol of mourning.

Samaria: The capital of the Northern Kingdom, also a region in the hill country of Palestine; conquered by Assyria in 721 or 722 B.C.

Satrap: Official title of governors of Persian provinces.

Seir, Mount: The chief mountain range in the territory of Edom.

Seleucus: The name of four of the Greek kings who ruled Syria and, at times, Palestine, from 312 B.C. to 129 B.C., who were part of the Seleucid dynasty.

Semite: A person who is from one of the groups of people who are descendants of Shem, the son of Noah, or who speaks one of a group of languages classified as Semitic (such groups include the Arabs, Arameans, Assyrians, Babylonians, Canaanites, Hebrews, and Phoenicians).

Senir: Amorite name for Mount Hermon, a snow-capped peak between the Sea of Galilee and Damascus.

Sheba: A famous trading nation in Arabia.

Shekel: In Old Testament times, a unit of weight (approximately .4 ounces); in New Testament times, a coin of the same weight.

Sheol: The abode of the dead.

Shinar: A name for Babylonia.

Shoa: A people whose exact identity is unknown, perhaps Aramean mercenaries in the army of Babylon.

Sibraim: A place on the northern border of Canaan between Damascus and Hamath.

Sidon: An ancient Phoenician seaport between Tyre and Beiruit; this city was an agricultural, fishing, and trading center famous for its purple dye which was made from the murex shell.

Simeon: One of the twelve tribes of Israel, descended from the second son of Jacob and Leah.

Sodom: A very wicked city, destroyed along with Gomorrah (see Genesis 19); now located under the southern part of the Dead Sea.

Susa: The capital of Elam, in southwest Iran; became the winter capital of the kings of Persia; honored by Shiite Muslims as the burial place of Daniel.

Syene: A trading village located at the southern end of Egypt.

Tamar: A fortress city in the extreme southeastern part of Judah near the southern end of the Dead Sea.

Tammuz: The Sumerian god of spring vegetation.

Tarshish: A far-off port that exported fine silver, tin, iron, and lead; perhaps another name for Sardinia or Tartessus, located in Spain.

Tehaphnehes: A city located on the eastern frontier in northern Egypt.

Tel-Abib: *Mound of the flood;* a community of exiled Israelites in Babylon; the name comes from the mound on which it was built; the mound was believed to have contained the ruins of a city which was there before the Flood.

Teman: Home of the Temanites, a clan descended from Esau; the largest city in central Edom.

Teraphim: Idols of various kinds; Ezekiel says the Babylonians used them in divination.

Thebes: Chief city of Upper (southern) Egypt.

Tyre: An important Phoenician seaport in southern Phoenicia; famous for its navigators and traders.

Tubal: A country in Asia Minor, famous for its metal working.

Ulai: A canal near Susa.

Zadok: A priest during the reign of David whose descendants gained control of the priesthood in the Jerusalem Temple.

Zebulun: One of the twelve tribes of Israel, descended from the tenth son of Jacob and Leah.

Zedad: A place on the northern border of Canaan.

Zedekiah: King of Judah from 597-587 B.C.; also the name of an exile, the son of Maaseiah, who was condemned by Jeremiah for false prophecy.

Zemer: A city in Lebanon.

Guide to Pronunciation

Abednego: Ah-BED-neh-go
Abomination: Ah-bah-mih-NAY-shun
Ahasuerus: Ah-hah-zoo-AIR-us
Akkadian: Ah-KAY-dee-an
Amasis: AM-ah-sis
Ammonites: AM-moh-nites
Amorite: AM-moh-rite
Antiochus: An-TIE-oh-kus
Apocalyptic: Ah-pah-kah-LIP-tic
Arabah: ARE-ah-bah
Arabia: Ah-RAY-bee-ah
Aramaic: Air-ah-MAY-ick
Arioch: ARE-ee-ock
Arvad: ARE-vahd
Ashpenaz: ASH-peh-noz
Assur: ASH-ur
Assyria: Ah-SEER-ee-ah
Astarte: As-TAR-teh
Azariah: As-eh-RYE-ah
Azzur: AZZ-ur
Baal-meon: Bah-ALL-may-AHN
Bamah: Bah-MAH
Bashan: Bah-SHAHN
Belshazzar: BELL-shah-zar
Benaiah: Beh-NIGH-ah
Berothah: Beh-ROH-thah
Beth-jeshimoth: BETH-yeh-shih-MOTHE

Beth-togarmah: BETH-toh-gar-MAH
Buzi: BU-zye
Canaanites: KAY-nah-nites
Canneh: CAN-neh
Cappadocia: Cah-pah-doh-SEE-ah
Carchemish: Car-SHEH-mish
Censer: SEN-ser
Chaldeans: Kal-DEE-ans
Chebar: CHAY-bar
Cherethites: CHAIR-eh-thites
Cherubim: CHER-ah-bim
Chilmad: KILL-mad
Cubit: CUE-bit
Cyprus: SIGH-pruss
Damascus: Duh-MASS-kus
Darius the Mede: Dah-RIE-us the MEED
Dedan: DEE-dan
Edom: EE-dum
Elam: EE-lum
Elishah: Eh-LIGH-shah
En-eglaim: En-eh-GLAH-eem
En-gedi: En-GEH-dee
Ephah: EE-fah
Ephraim: Ee-frah-EEM
Eschatological: Ess-kat-ah-LAH-jih-cal
Ethiopia: Ee-thee-OH-pia
Ezekiel Ben-adam: Ee-ZEE-kee-al BEN-ah-DAHM
Gamad: GAY-mad
Gebal: Gay-BALL
Gedeliah: Geh-dah-LIGH-ah
Gilead: GIH-lee-ad
Gomer: GO-mer
Hamonah: Hah-mo-NAH
Hamon-gog: Hay-mahn-GOG
Hananiah: Han-nah-NIGH-ah
Haran: Ha-RAHN
Hauran: HAWR-ahn

Hazar-enon: Hah-ZAR-eh-NON
Hazer-hatticon: Ha-ZER-hah-tee-KAHN
Helbon: HEL-bon
Helech: HEH-leck
Hethlon: HETH-lon
Hin: Hihn
Hittites: HIT-tites
Homer: HO-mer
Hophra: HOFF-rah
Issachar: IZ-zah-car
Jaazaniah: Jah-az-ah-NIGH-ah
Javan: JAH-van
Jehoiachin: Jeh-HOY-ah-kin
Jehoiakim: Jeh-HOY-ah-kim
Kabod: Kah-BODE
Kedar: KEH-dar
Kiriathaim: Keer-ee-ah-THIGH-im
Koa: KO-ah
Leviathan: Leh-VIGH-ah-thun
Lud: LOOD
Magog: MAH-gog
Manasseh: Mah-NAS-seh
Medes: MEEDS
Mene: MEN-eh
Meribath-kadesh: MER-ih-bath-KAH-desh
Meshach: MEE-shack
Mesopotamia: Mes-soh-poh-TAY-mee-uh
Migdol: MIG-dole
Mishael: MISH-ah-el
Moab: MOH-ab
Nabonidus: Nab-boh-NIGH-dus
Nabopolasser: Nab-boh-poh-LASS-er
Naphtali: Naf-TAL-lee
Nebuchadnezzar: Neh-buh-kahd-NEZ-zer
Nebuchadrezzar: Neh-buh-kahd-DREZ-zer
Negeb: NEH-gheb
Nisan: Knee-SAHN

Oholah: Oh-ho-LAH
Oholibah: Oh-ho-lee-BAH
Onias: Oh-NIGH-us
Parsin: PAR-sin
Pathros: PATH-ros
Pelatiah: Pel-eh-TIGH-ah
Pelusium: Pih-LOO-see-um
Philistia: Fih-LISS-tee-ah
Philistines: FILL-is-teens
Phoenicia: Foh-KNEE-shuh
Pibeseth: Pi-BEH-seth
Prefect: PREE-fect
Ptolemy: TOH-leh-mee
Put: PUT
Raamah: Rah-ah-MAH
Rabbah: Rah-BAH
Reuben: ROO-ben
Rhodes: ROADS
Riblah: RIB-lah
Samaria: Sah-MARE-ee-ah
Satrap: SAT-trap
Seir: Seh-EER
Seleucus: Seh-LOO-sus
Selucids: Seh-LOO-sids
Senir: Seh-NEAR
Shadrach: SHAD-rack
Shaphan: SHAH-fahn
Sheba: SHE-bah
Shekel: SHECK-el
Sheol: SHE-ole
Shinar: SHIH-nar
Shoa: SHOW-ah
Sibraim: Sib-RAY-im
Sidon: SIGH-dun
Simeon: SIM-ee-un
Sodom: SOD-um
Susa: SUE-zah

Syene: Sigh-EEN
Tamar: TAY-mar
Tammuz: Tah-MUZ
Tarshish: Tar-SHEESH
Tehaphnehes: Teh-HOFF-neh-hees
Tekel: TEH-kel
Tel-abib: Tell-ah-BEEB
Teman: TAY-man
Teraphim: TER-ah-fim
Thebes: THEE-bes
Tigris-Euphrates: TIGH-griss-you-FRAY-tees
Tyre: TIRE
Tubal: TOO-bal
Ulai: YOU-lie
Uphaz: YOU-faz
Uzal: YOU-zal
Zadok: ZAY-dock
Zebulun: ZEB-you-lun
Zedad: ZEE-dad
Zedekiah: Zeh-deh-KIGH-uh
Zemer: ZEH-mer
Zoan: ZOE-an

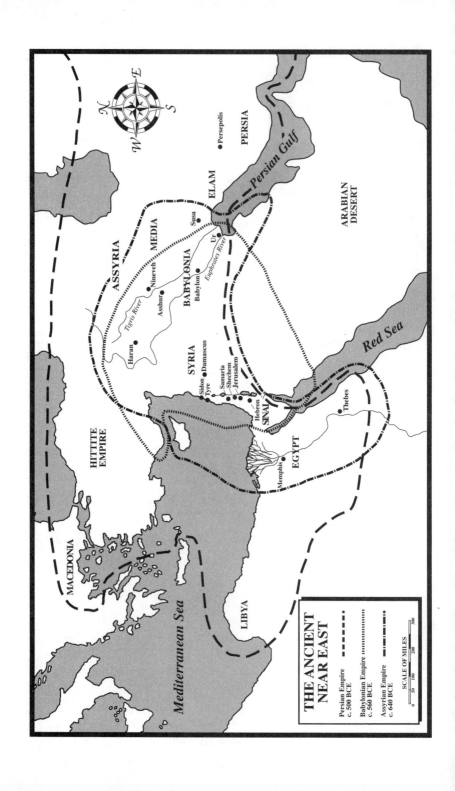

THE ANCIENT
NEAR EAST

Persian Empire
c. 500 BCE

Babylonian Empire
c. 560 BCE

Assyrian Empire
c. 640 BCE

SCALE OF MILES

0   50 100   200   300

THE KINGDOMS OF ISRAEL AND JUDAH

SCALE OF MILES
0   10   20   30   40

Damascus

Sidon

KINGDOM OF DAMASCUS

Tyre

PHOENICIA

Dan

ISRAEL

SAMARIA

River Jordan

The Great Sea

Joppa

Bethel

AMMON

JERUSALEM

Tokea

Gaza

Moresheth

PHILISTIA

Lake Asphaltitis (Dead Sea)

JUDAH

Beersheba

MOAB

Arabian Desert

Kadesh-barnea

EDOM

KINGDOM OF EGYPT

Elath

N
W   E
S